The Christy Quest

Self Portrait by Howard Chandler Christy

The Christy Quest

HELEN F. COPLEY

Be glad of life because it gives you the chance to love and work, to play and to look up at the stars.

– Henry Van Dyke

THE PATRICE PRESS
TUCSON, ARIZONA

Library of Congress Cataloging-in-Publication Data
Copley, Helen F., 1935-
The Christy quest / Helen F. Copley.
p. cm.
ISBN: 1-880397-30-7
1. Christy, Howard Chandler, 1873-1952. 2. Illustrators—United States Biography. 3. Copley, Helen F., 1935-
I. Title.
N6537.C4973C65 1999
760'. 092—dc21 99-34825
[B] CIP

Cover design by Randy Presson, ECCO Design & Communications, Dallas, Texas; eccodesign.com

The Patrice Press
P. O. Box 83659
Tucson AZ 85754
patricepress.com
1/800/367-9242

For David and Carol Ann

Sometimes, with luck,
we find the kind of true friend,
male or female,
that appears only two or three times
in a lucky lifetime,
one that will winter us and summer us,
grieve, rejoice, and travel with us. . . .
– Barbara Holland

The author at Christy's boyhood desk.

Preface

"How can you *not* write about this?" my friends questioned. "Look at what has happened, look at all the coincidences that keep coming. Tell the story from the beginning." Each time a friend asked, "What's the latest in the quest?" I attempted to describe the most recent occurrence, but I found that I could not do so without bringing in other names, faces, and events. Everything was integrally meshed. One thread consistently led to another.

"I'll get to it one of these days," I thought. As I attained each step on my quest I expected it to be over. Instead, I felt as compelled as ever to continue. The adventure had become tightly woven into my life. It was a part of "me" and I enjoyed it too much to give it up.

I visited the Christy haunts in New York and Ohio; went to the Gilcrease Museum in Tulsa, Oklahoma (finding a cache of Christy portraits and works in oil there), went to St. Simon's Island in Georgia and White Springs, Florida; visited Hawaii, (where I unexpectedly discovered the Fannie Hurst connection); went to Los Angeles, Washington, D.C., Annapolis, Md., and the many other sites and scenes which often unexpectedly had produced Christy signposts.

The momentum escalated when I began hearing from others who, after seeing my ad in newspapers around the country, shared their interest in the artist.

I began to ask myself, "Why *not* put the story on paper?" The seed had been planted and ideas germinated. "Okay," I mused, "at least I have a title—*The Christy Quest*—and that's a beginning."

I picked up a notepad and wrote out those three words. Then came a first sentence. It surprised me. I was back in Utah, on a skiing trip. I saw the lodge clearly. I breathed the cold air of the mountain resort. The chill was unmistakable, as was the pain which stirred below the surface of my mind.

With the memory of the scene came feelings, long dormant but incredibly intense. I had learned through years of trial and error that pushing away feelings was no good. They insisted on expression either in the present, or later, and usually gained power through repression. So I sat, pen in hand, and allowed the grief and fear to emerge.

I continued to write, thoroughly miserable. Then "Gamaliel" came to mind—the guiding angel who appeared to me early in the quest. Some inner shift occurred and I felt lighter. Hope again was offered. "Maybe," I thought, "maybe I *can* write about these experiences for whatever reason or purpose."

It was obvious that I had unconsciously held onto pain. I had read many times of the catharsis of writing. "I'll try," I promised myself. "I'll give it a chance. If the story's just for me, that's okay too." I relaxed somewhat, breathing easier, slower, and let the words come.

I was unable to write for long stretches of time. I could write every day, or several times a day, but the paragraphs ended with each separate experience. I decided to accept this episodic form as the most comfortable way for me to get the Christy story on paper.

When I tried to force the writing, to lengthen it or blend one happening into the next occurrence, the words stubbornly refused to come. Some excerpts were longer than others, but most came forth curiously concise. They would not expand, even to an additional comma.

I visited bookstores, searching for a quick "how-to-write-a-book" message. The wealth of information offered was overwhelming. Time after time, I walked out of the store intimidated and confused. This pursuit didn't feel right, and I was becoming rigid with anxiety.

I prayed for help and kept on writing. My dear companion David, as always, was a staunch supporter when my resolve waned. "You'll feel better when you see what it looks like in print. Give it some time. It'll come together."

I'd had one high school typing class and only one brief secretarial experience after college. I was dismally unprepared for the mechanics of writing. I needed a typist and praying for one to appear, I waited.

"Aren't you about ready to get some of that into print?" David asked, eyeing my notebook thoughtfully. I had been writing for several weeks by then.

"Well, yes, I guess so," I answered, "but I haven't found a typist yet." I thumbed through the sheets. "I wonder if anyone can even translate my writing?"

David grinned and shrugged. "No problem. You already *have* someone to type it. Rhonda said she'd be glad to do it."

Rhonda Morgan was David's secretarial right arm and had been in that position for years. Her talents were legendary, her skills awesome. David always spoke highly of her.

"But, David, wait a minute," I argued back, "Rhonda is busy with *your* work. How can she take on anything else? And she has two children to raise, and a husband—"

David interrupted firmly, "She's so fast she'll breeze through it. And she wants to do it." He paused, letting the words sink in. "As far as transcribing it, if you're worried about that, read it off onto tape and send that to her. I do that all the time. She's used to it."

I knew that I could never find anyone I might trust or enjoy working with more than Rhonda. I knew her warmth and gracious spirit firsthand. It was, one more time, an example of simplicity. Rhonda was already in my life. No search for a typist was necessary.

"I'd love it." I smiled at David, handing him the yellow sheets, "It's a perfect solution." And so the book began.

—Helen Copley
Dallas, Texas
Spring 1999

1

I first saw the painting called *The Christ* on the cover of a book in December 1984. The book had been suggested to me by a friend. It was called *Forgiveness and Jesus* and had been written by *Course in Miracles* scholar Kenneth Wapnick. I happened to see it while browsing in a neighborhood bookstore near Southern Methodist University in Dallas. I bought it out of idle curiosity and began reading it at once, keeping it on my bedside table.

In the introduction Wapnick described the history of the painting. A color slide had been given to him by a professor, Dr. Martin Marchetta, and he had been so inspired that he chose it for the cover of his book. The original work could not be found.

I studied the picture. It was arresting. Suddenly—for the first time in my life—I felt as though I was looking at the *man* called Jesus. He was a real person! Energy and warmth flowed from the painting, as if it were alive. Jesus seemed to be present—breathing, immediate and intimate. The face I saw was tender, yet possessed great strength. Strangely, to me there was an unfinished "feel" about the image, yet it also seemed solid and complete, with nothing left out, a whole. I dimly recognized the artist's name, Howard Chandler Christy, but couldn't remember why or where I'd heard of him.

Weeks passed. I enjoyed Wapnick's book and read from it most evenings. I was also studying the *Course in Miracles*. The *Course* has been described as a psycho-spiritual plan, a path to inner peace. It is a simple technique: a lesson-a-day is provided for one year.

Three friends had told me about the *Course*. One had studied it consistently, one was in her first year of study, and one wished to embark on it. I decided to explore my friends' suggestion that I study it too. It seemed that I was meeting a mention of it at every turn.

Rather sheepishly I bought the three-volume set some days later. I had little experience with "New Age" thinking, being rather strictly raised in a traditional Protestant denomination. I felt distrustful of it. And here was the set of books I wanted to buy smack in the middle of the New Age section. I walked down the aisle almost furtively and paid for the books as quickly as I could, hoping no one I knew would see me.

I was half-skeptical and half-afraid to open the books at all. But I decided to peek at the thinnest volume of the three, which was titled, *The Teacher's Manual*, thinking, "Oh, well, why not!" I let the book fall open at its own will, shut my eyes, and placed a fingertip somewhere on the page.

"If there is some message here for me, then let me find it—or not," I whispered.

I began to read, "Look up and see His Word among the stars, where he has set your name along with His. Look up and find your certain destiny the world would hide but God would have you see. . . ."

Suddenly a picture flashed across the page—a scene from childhood I hadn't thought about in a long time. My eyes blurred, tears came quickly. I had wondered for years at the meaning of the most vivid spiritual experience I had ever had. Here were the words printed out before me describing what I had seen then, in the night sky, spelled out by stars: J-E-S-U-S.

I was six years old at the time, just beginning to read, but that name I knew from Bible story books and Sunday School lessons. Gradually, the entire scene played out before me. I saw myself, wearing a robe and ready for bed, sitting by myself on the curb in front of our house. I don't know why I went outside. I remember how quiet it seemed, looking up at the dark night sky filled with

The Christ

stars. I saw the Milky Way.

Then I watched in fascination as the largest stars shifted and moved around to print out in huge letters the name *Jesus*. The word took up almost the entire sky. I wasn't afraid. I simply sat and stared.

I have no idea how long I was there. Abruptly, as though waking up from a dream, I sensed my mother bending over me, shaking me by both shoulders. She looked frightened. "What's wrong? What is it? Wake up," she kept saying. I tried to explain that I hadn't heard her calling to me at all. Yet I remember thinking even then, as strange as it was, that I would never forget it. Somehow, even though I didn't understand what had happened, I knew it had been a gift. I never spoke of it again.

I thought about it frequently, however, then and as I grew older. But slowly, the memory faded, re-emerging only rarely throughout my adult life. Until now.

At this same time, I began to dream of *The Christ* painting while I slept and to think about it during the day. I was intrigued and longed to see the original.

I looked for information on Christy, the artist. I had almost no luck. The more avenues I tried, the less I discovered. It seemed that little had been written about him, other than a few sparse biographical notes. Occasionally I found a brief reference to his work or, even more rarely, a reproduction of a painting. I was frustrated, and yet I couldn't stop searching.

Several months passed. The face of Christ and the need to find out more about the artist stayed with me. In fact, it was growing into a mild obsession. I visited libraries, book stores, art galleries, and magazine stands. After one particularly disappointing day, I was ready to give up. I didn't understand why I felt so compelled to learn something about Christy, and I was angry, disappointed, and confused because I had failed.

Tiredly, I wrote the name "Christy" on a piece of paper, put it in my billfold, and asked for help. "If I'm supposed to find this painting, then please do this for me," I prayed. Immediately, I felt relieved. The belief, the certainty that I would be successful surprised me with its immediacy. I relaxed at once and the nagging sense of urgency disappeared.

At the same time, I was reading the *Course in Miracles* textbook as best I could, though it was often difficult to understand. I began to experience profound discomfort as old ideas, rooted in years of tradition and habit, began to crumble and fall away.

It was an "up and down" time. Yet, despite the emotional upheaval, I continued to read and pursue this *Course*. A place deep within me, or a part of myself, had begun to open. I knew there was no turning back.

The machinery of this process moved at its own pace. My life continued as before, ebbing and flowing in its own rhythm. My mind and heart were centered on a continuing struggle to keep afloat of one personal crisis after another.

I could not hide from the fact that the structure of my life was breaking apart. I had been married for almost thirty years. I was fifty years old. A divorce and its consequences seemed unthinkable, yet its inevitability became clearer each day.

I tried to ride the waves of change as best I could. My three children were caught up in challenges of their own. I found it hard not to carry their burdens as well. I was losing my old identity. At the same time, the emptiness created by the loss of old ideas and familiar comforts gave space to new ways of experiencing. I began to turn to a part of myself I had not been in touch with. Although it was a frightening time, it was also, occasionally and surprisingly, an exhilarating one. I prayed deeply for a guide, a mentor or teacher—someone I might turn to with questions I had never before asked.

My "faith" had been patterned in traditional religion. I was born to strong Methodist parents, a mother and father whose lives were anchored in "the church." I not only accepted, but grew to depend on this structure. It was a way of life that worked in my world. When there were questions or fears, I stoutly forced them out of my mind. Now these long pushed-under doubts surfaced, pleading for not only attention, but my own survival. As one cherished concept after another fell away, the "I" I had known was also dying. Into this void came the gift of what I began to call "The Christy Quest."

It brought with it a refreshing sense of adventure, giving my torn mind something to cling to. I eagerly grasped this "life preserver" in waters of grief. When I focused on the magic of the search, I could sense, even in a physical way, a warmth of healing, as if to say, "There is more." Hope, I suppose, as Emily Dickinson's timid bird, alit on my shoulder.

In the midst of this turmoil, we went on a ski trip to Deer Valley, Utah—my husband, children and I. It was a particularly difficult time. The challenge of continuing a painful marriage was often overwhelming. I was tired, frightened, and struggling for guidance, for a resolution, an "answer." Sleep was difficult and fitful. There were dreams, snatches of pictures and images throughout the nights.

I awoke one such morning, knowing that something had printed out in my mind, a piece of information. I lay still, trying to remember whatever dream had presented itself. One word appeared. Simultaneously I both saw it and heard it. The word (or name, as I later realized) was "Gamaliel." It rang a tiny note in my mind, but there the identity ceased. I knew it must be important, as it had been so clear. Surprisingly, I felt calmer and more refreshed than I had in weeks. I decided to be as open-minded as possible, allowing myself to expect a definition or an explanation and then to believe in it.

"Gamaliel." Could it be a Biblical name? I found a Gideon Bible in the bedside table, thumbed through it, and finally hit upon an excerpt from Acts regarding Paul's teacher, the respected Pharisee, Gamaliel. I couldn't imagine how any part of this passage related to my circumstances, and yet I knew heartwise that a key for me lay in the words. And by now I knew that in time I would discover whatever message the name implied. I waited and I trusted.

Early in my search for Christy, I had explored the standard reference books on the shelves at home. The first and most obvious was the Columbia Encyclopedia. I turned to C-H-R-I-S-T-Y and found, not Howard Chandler, but Sir James Barrie, the name ending not in "y", but in "ie."

This energetic Englishman had founded what is now the famous auction house, known worldwide as Christie's. I was disappointed to find nothing about my new artist-friend, but became interested in the history of Sir James' venerable business. I had been to London several times and had passed the impressive, stately doors of Christie's, wanting to walk inside. I envisioned the display of magnificent antiques laid out in British splendor, room after room of them. I knew there were branches of Christie's in many cities, one of which was New York. Perhaps one day I might visit it. An enticing idea.

This was pure serendipity—I had looked for one name and had found another. I knew there must be some connection, or more correctly, I sensed it. I anticipated that another clue was coming.

I had not long to wait. My husband came home from work that evening, smiling, with an invitation which had arrived earlier in the day. The manager of the New York branch of Christie's would be in Dallas the next day and we, among others, were asked to attend a welcoming dinner for him. Did I want to go? I felt a surge of joy and gratitude.

Throughout the next day I was nervous and anxious, but happy. The hours dragged until eight o'clock.

At last, all were gathered and the guest of honor arrived. Christopher Burge was tall and slim, erudite and very English, charming and warm. He moved from group to group easily, chatting and chuckling. He was a young man, yet possessed mature confidence and a seasoned wit. Soon we moved to our tables, guided by the arrangement of placecards.

I was thrilled to see my name next to his. During the meal, he spoke of his life in England, and the challenges and adjustments of his move to New York. There were queries from all, and he graciously answered each one. At the first opportunity, I asked him if he'd heard of an American artist named Howard Chand—

Before I could finish the name he grinned and said, "Christy, of course. We have auctioned many of his paintings."

I explained my growing fascination with the artist. Christopher seemed genuinely interested and offered to help. He told me that catalogs, books, and prints were available and he would send more information when he returned to New York. He also invited me to tour the Christie galleries.

The evening ended too quickly, at least for me. As I thanked Christopher for his help, he said, "You must go to a wonderful restaurant when you're in town. It's my favorite in New York. The walls are covered with Christy paintings, beautiful nude figures. It is called the Café des Artistes."

And so, for the first time, I heard the name of a place that would impact my life dramatically. Without realizing it, I had taken another step on my journey: #1 W. 67th St., New York City. The Hotel des Artistes.

2

While still on the first leg of my search, I began to experience an urge, an insistent and specific inner prompting to go to the Biblical Arts Center in Dallas. The center was easily accessible. It is located on a much-traveled route which I took almost daily, yet I stubbornly refused to heed this guidance. I kept thinking, I've already been there many times!

The Biblical Arts Center had always been a special place for me, fascinating, inspiring, and uplifting. It had been created in 1981 to house a huge painting called *The Miracle at Pentecos*t. A member of our church, the artist Torger Thompson, had conceived the idea for the painting and had carried it onto canvas over a long period. The execution of this giant creative endeavor was, in itself, miraculous. Hundreds of people stopped by his studio in a large warehouse to watch Thompson at work as the painting progressed.

Eventually the canvas began to assume a life of its own. Tales and stories of miracles that the painting was linked to emerged, were told and retold. In time, a large-scale reproduction of the Jerusalem Gate was constructed to house the painting. Its original warehouse home was then transformed into a spacious museum. A light-and-sound show to accompany and enhance the painting was added.

The Biblical Arts Center in Dallas

The museum now houses fine works of religious art, plus affording space for monthly exhibits. These changing displays often give new, untried artists an opportunity to show their work. Concerts, lectures, slide presentations, and tours are offered. A replica of the Garden Tomb in Jerusalem was built inside the courtyard.

Over the years I visited the museum often. I enjoyed taking out-of-town visitors there, or simply spending a peaceful hour wandering its quiet halls. Although I had not visited the center in more than a year, I felt I knew it well. I could not imagine a Christy connection there.

However, the voice persisted. Finally, almost angrily, I surrendered as I was on my way to my mother's house. I turned into the parking lot, slammed the car door, and marched up the few steps to the giant wooden entry gates. I had a few minutes to spare before my scheduled visit with my mother, and I planned to take only a half-dozen steps inside, quickly wheel around, and go on with my plans for the day. I didn't want to be late. On this particular afternoon, I had something important to show Mother. But first I would get this "voice" business out of the way once and for all.

I raced through the foyer, glancing around the courtyard walls where familiar paintings hung. Perhaps, I thought, as long as I was inside, I should give a few minutes to the current exhibit and then, of course, leave. Almost immediately I found myself standing in front of the Garden Tomb in the courtyard.

My mind seemed to shut down, the constant mental chattering suddenly ceased. I became aware of not another sound, but the lack of it. There was utter silence. I realized that I was alone in the room—there were no other visitors, no staff members, no museum guides, no voices, no footsteps, nothing.

Only the quiet.

But I didn't feel alone.

I became aware of a great peace—a sense of serenity, a feeling of "rightness" and purpose. I turned. It was almost as if physical hands pivoted me toward the left. I stood staring at a huge painting I had never seen before. A magnificent rendition of the birth of Christ covered almost the entire wall. A loving Mary held the baby, while Joseph, the shepherds, animals, and angels watched in reverence. It was a familiar scene, certainly, but it was portrayed with such gentle power and artistic beauty, I was left breathless.

I walked closer, as though drawn by the painting's magnetic energy. It was titled *Peace on Earth.* I studied the scene for some minutes, filled with gratitude for such a visual and emotional gift. And in my haste, I had almost missed it! I wondered, finally, who the artist was, who the creator of such a work of love could be. My eyes traveled down to the lower right hand corner and I saw a signature: Christy.

For a moment I didn't recognize the name. And then I saw "Howard Chandler" and I knew. I had methodically, at times grimly, plodded through library stacks, pursued information in book stores, and searched for paintings in many marble-halled museums, when all the while, this Christy masterpiece was here, in a most familiar setting, ten minutes from my home. I had been "told," over and over, to come here. I pledged, at that moment, to henceforth trust this voice within.

Immediately, something caught my attention down the hall, some sound or movement. I turned to look at another large canvas. It was a second painting, unmistakably a Christy. As I drew closer, I read its title, *The Resurrection*. Inspiring and majestic, the angel, sword in hand, was bathed in light. Why and when had these paintings come here? Where had they come from? I looked back to the reception desk and saw a museum guide.

I went to her, filled with curiosity. She called the curator from his office. He explained to me that the paintings had arrived about a year ago. They had been sent by an anonymous donor after being discovered in the artist's studio in New York City. They had never left the studio before coming here.

A young woman named Jennifer joined us. She served as librarian and historian for the center. She spoke of their joy in receiving not one but two fine works of art, an unexpected offer that came "out of the blue." The donors had insisted on anonymity. The couple's name was never, for any reason, to be revealed. No photographs could be taken of the paintings. And if these conditions were violated, the paintings would be immediately returned to New York. The museum, thrilled at the gift, agreed to the terms.

The mystery was intriguing. Why such secrecy? Jennifer broke in, stating that Christy was a mystery figure himself. He was famed for his lusty approach to life, which he expressed on canvas with beautiful, nude models. Combining naivete and sensuality, the Christy Girls had been a pictorial vanguard of feminine freedom. Of all artists, why had *he* chosen to paint these two powerful religious works?

These spiritual paintings were conceived in the last decade of his life. What had happened to him? Why had he changed his focus?

"Well," Jennifer sighed, "at least we know he painted these two pieces—the only ones of this nature he ever executed." I paused. Something was tugging at my mind.

"Wait," I said. "He did another religious painting, a third one." They politely but resolutely disagreed. And then I remembered what I was bringing to my mother. It was the book, *Forgiveness and Jesus* with *The Christ* pictured on the cover.

"I have a copy of the painting with me, in my car," I announced, and hurried out to retrieve it. They were amazed when they saw it and immediately made photocopies for their files.

As I drove away, I realized that this day was the only time I had taken the book from my house. Synchronicity or "grace" had unmistakably appeared. It was perfect timing, a concept I would appreciate more and more in the years ahead.

Suddenly I looked forward to this journey, as it would continue to unfold. I was "questing," and I loved it.

I don't remember how many days had passed from the moment I wrote "Christy" on the slip of paper as an act of surrender—or as a plea for help, until the time of the discovery of the painting. But I am certain that it was no longer than a week before I spied the book again in my neighborhood bookstore.

The cover caught my eye, because the color looked a bit different. The painting on the first edition had a bluish cast. This one was golden. I was puzzled and picked up the book to examine it. Turning to the inside front cover, I read, "Edition II." I flipped to the last page of the introduction and scanned down to the final paragraph which happily announced the location of "the lost Christ." It was owned by the Methodist Church, or its publishing arm, Abingdon Press, and resided in their offices in Nashville, Tennessee.

At first I was stunned. I took the book to the sales clerk, paid for it, went back to my car, and drove home. I realized that my request had been answered. The painting had surfaced after forty-four years. I was, as the minutes and hours passed, increasingly thankful. Gratitude blossomed into awe. I had prayed for a miracle but hadn't expected it to come so quickly, so easily, and therefore, for me at least, so dramatically. I had experienced many miracles, or expressions of love, throughout the years, but somehow this seemed different. Tiny electric thrills shot through me. I was developing a healthy respect for this "power" which had touched my life.

A short time later, I took the new edition of the book to the Biblical Arts Center. They, too, had tried to research the painting and/or its whereabouts with no luck. We rejoiced together at the discovery. I felt that, in time, I would go to Nashville for a first-hand view of Christy's work. I believed for some days afterward that this particular quest had ended. I would dismiss it from my thinking and go on to whatever adventure Life next offered.

But I couldn't stop pondering what had happened. I knew there was more to the search. It was far from finished.

I went back for another look at the Biblical Arts paintings. "What am I to do next?" I wondered as I stood before *Peace on Earth*. "Help me," I almost spoke aloud. "What is this inner push, this constant unrest?"

I heard Jennifer enter the foyer and as I turned toward her, I knew what the next step would be.

"What do you think about asking the Methodist Church to send the painting here to the museum to join the other two?" I asked. Before she could reply, I heard myself saying, "It's supposed to be here. I know it is."

Jennifer looked from me to the Nativity and back again, "I think you're right. It's a wonderful idea," she said.

Having once voiced the thought, I was aflame with the prospect of bringing *The Christ* to Dallas. For whatever reasons, it had been closeted from the public for too long. Now, perhaps, it might be exhibited and could serve as an inspiration to all who saw it. And what an ideal place for its "resurrection!" I marveled at the perfection of this setting and the power of the painting.

Jennifer promised to contact Abingdon Press as soon as possible. We promised to keep in close touch. My mind warned me not to expect too much, but my heart overruled reason and continued its song of thanks. I knew that the painting would come. Once again, I waited.

I spoke with Jennifer several times during the month following the decision to request the loan of Christy's portrait of Christ. As with most negotiations, time was needed for the necessary correspondence, legal matters, insurance, and so forth.

One morning I drove home from an errand, turned the corner toward my driveway and "knew" that there would be important news waiting. My message center had two brief sentences recorded. Jennifer's voice said, "Helen, you must come. We have just hung the painting!"

With the arrival of *The Christ*, my private clouds began to lift. I went many times to stand before its healing presence. I loved to watch others pause and study the painting, "Look how the eyes move following from side to side. He looks so real."

The painting remained at the center for three years. I suppose thousands must have seen it. It hung on a wall beside the huge painted portrayal of the empty tomb, with the angel as guardian.

I marveled that the painting was actually changing my life. I felt hope and a new kind of faith, a developing belief in life's goodness and purpose. That purpose had touched me in this surprising way and I was grateful.

I knew from overhearing the whispered conversations and from seeing quiet light in the faces of those who stopped to view Christy's image of the man called Jesus, that other spirits, too, were touched. Many stood in a silence that was almost stronger than words, rapt and attentive.

One day while I strolled through the center, it occurred to me that I hadn't paid much attention to Thompson's *Miracle* painting in a long time. I walked down the back hall leading to the display room in which the artist's sketches, brushes, paint tubes, and photographs were exhibited.

This whole thing is about miracles, I thought as I entered. "Torg," as he was affectionately referred to by all who knew him, was a miracle-maker indeed. A simple and unassuming commercial artist, he felt the God-sent "tap on the shoulder" and humbly began to create his masterpiece.

He was guided to choose as his subject the biblical bestowal of Spirit during Pentecost. More than one hundred figures are portrayed in his painting, each of whom had in some way been personally touched by Jesus. A diagram of these figures lay at the side of the room in a display case I hadn't seen before. I glanced curiously into it and began to read the names printed below the chart.

From left to right there appeared the disciples, the moneychangers, the lepers healed by Christ, Mary and Martha, and Lazarus. Peter was prominent—the flame of Pentecost bright above his head, shouting out his intense joy. As my eyes traveled to the right edge of the case, I heard, once again, the name "Gamaliel." I read further down the list and was shocked to see that name in print.

Paul and his respected Pharisee teacher, Gamaliel, stand far off to the side, talking together and watching the excitement playing out before them. But something didn't quite fit.

"What's going on here?" I asked. "When and how were Jesus and Gamaliel together?" Why did it seem so strange to see him in the painting?

I hurried to find Jennifer. She told me that some years ago, Torg had visited Forest Lawn, the beautiful cemetery in Los Angeles, and had been deeply moved by the huge painting called *The Crucifixion* by Jan Styka. The Polish artist's giant canvas had inspired Thompson to continue to believe in his own vision. It could be done—a great painting of splendid proportion could be created. And that creation would praise God by inspiring those who saw it.

Torg studied Styka's work in detail. It was the moment before the crucifixion. Jesus stands gazing at the cross, surrounded by scattered groups along and upon the hillside. Torg was surprised to see Gamaliel there, but, he vowed, if Styka chose to place him with the others, then he, too, would include the rabbi in his painting. And with the teacher, he also placed Paul, the firebrand student.

I knew then, as I had sensed months earlier at the ski lodge in Utah, that Gamaliel was a teacher, or guide, for me as well. Here were Christy and Gamaliel together at this place, which might not have been constructed had it not been for Jan Styka's influence on Torg.

I went home, took out my Bible, and began re-reading the excerpt from Acts 5, where the strict Pharisee Gamaliel defends Peter and John for preaching the Messiahship of Jesus in the temple. Gamaliel said, "Keep away from these men and let them alone; for if this plan or this undertaking is of men, it will fail; but if it is of God, you will not be able to overthrow them."

What possible meaning could that have for me?

At first, back in Utah, the words meant little, either to the circumstances of my life or to the meaning of the Christy Quest. My mind toyed with the passage. I kept trying to analyze it, getting nowhere. Finally giving up in frustration, I shut the Bible and put it back into its bookcase slot.

I guess if I'm supposed to get some message, it will come when the time is right, I thought, halfheartedly. In the months that followed, the words scarcely crossed my mind. My life was busy, and I told myself that I had no time for further confusion.

After I rediscovered Gamaliel, the words began to make sense. The wise judge, Gamaliel, advised his Jewish council to make no hasty judgment against the disciples. "Let time and events prove the truth," he counseled. Suddenly I realized that the words were exactly what I needed to hear.

"Relax—whatever is meant to happen will surely occur," spoke the words. The concept was familiar, but I seemed to receive it in a new and different way. I breathed deeply, aware of a healing sense of lightness, as if an unknown burden had been shed.

"I really don't have to figure any of this out," I realized, "and I don't have to judge it as right or wrong, or good or bad, either. I don't have to force anything. Perhaps, just as this message has come, so will other answers. I'll know what to do. The guidance will be there at the perfect time." I marveled at the simplicity of the idea.

"So this is what 'Truth' means," I thought. "It covers every situation. It is universal, all-encompassing, and yet astoundingly simple." I decided to trust this process, allowing Life to unfold as it would. No fight, no resistance. What a relief!

"If I am meant to live on my own, then that will happen. Or not," I mused. "So will the Christy adventure continue, or not." I thanked Gamaliel for what was, for me, at that moment, such a powerful guideline. Once again, I would wait, but with a far stronger faith. The future beckoned with much less anxiety, and the nature of the "quest" took on a new sense of freedom.

Eventually the Christy Quest became ever more secular, as if I were retracing Christy's life in reverse. I began with his profound spirituality and moved through his equally profound attachment to the earth and its pleasures, until at last I grasped that there was no line of demarcation between the two worlds, earthly and spiritual. Both were of the same piece.

3

For more than a year little happened in the Christy Quest, but my life had changed dramatically. My marriage had ended. For a while I continued to live in our family home, although the children had grown up and moved on into their own lives. As time passed, I realized that I, too, was ready to move into a new environment. I began to think of a place of my own, a smaller home or apartment.

I immediately found, through a friend's suggestion, a townhouse which had just been put on the market. It seemed perfect. I loved it from my first step inside and made a down payment at once, moving in a few months later. I was delighted that I didn't have to "look" for a home—it simply appeared as a gift.

I had never lived on my own before, and I found the experience one of joy. There were, of course, challenges and innumerable new things to learn, yet help was always provided and the transition was far easier than I dared hope.

Still, I often forced myself to attend to the concerns of the day through a haze of anxiety. I fought sinking into a depression framed by doubt and indecision. I had found spiritual guidance in the *Course in Miracles*, but I longed for someone to talk to about the changes I was experiencing. The perplexing "whys" continued to nag at me. I couldn't understand the unrest the Christy

Quest was causing.

One day a friend called to tell me that I had been on her mind. She felt guided to suggest I get in touch with a friend of hers, a counselor whom she felt was very gifted. "Tarran Caldwell is a wonderful listener and very loving."

I decided almost at once to call her. We made arrangements to meet at her home.

"What's your address?" I asked.

"I live on a street called Christy," said Tarran. My heart stopped.

"You won't believe this," I said. "The name of your street is a large part of the reason I want to talk to you!"

Several days later, I drove out to Christy Lane. I rang the doorbell. After a few moments, the door was opened by her cheerful husband David. He held out his hand, warmly shaking mine, and I felt at home.

Tarran seemed filled with light. The room radiated and responded to her presence. So did I. She had a Madonna-like appearance. She might have strolled out of a Titian canvas. Or more like a Rubens' angel, I mused. An abundance of auburn ringlets haloed her face, springing down to her shoulders. From the first moment of greeting, I experienced a joyous connection.

In her office we settled into comfortable chairs. She was also an artist. I glanced around the room. Several of her paintings were displayed. They seemed filled with the same serenity which emanated from her.

David tapped lightly on the door. "Sorry. I left the book I've been reading in here. I'll just grab it and be off." He retrieved the paperback from an end table and turned to leave the room. At the door, he paused and held up the book, asking if I had ever heard of either it or the author. "The writer's name is Ken Wapnick," he explained. I was speechless. The book was *Forgiveness and Jesus.* The cover painting was, of course, *The Christ* by Howard Chandler Christy.

"That's the reason I'm here," I said. The synchronicity of the moment overwhelmed us. I felt an electric charge. I knew that a Power and a Purpose had brought us here together.

I told Tarran about the Christy connection, talking for two hours. At last I no longer felt so alone or so strange. Tarran shared her own spiritual struggles, her doubts and fears, as well as the miracles, giving me the space to do so as well.

As I hugged Tarran a grateful good-bye, I felt that a new sense of adventure had been born. I walked toward my car with a feeling of hope. The air rang with energy. I turned and waved good-bye again. The sun beamed down in typical Texas summer intensity.

Thunderheads were billowing above, and lightning flashed between the clouds. I climbed into my car and felt the pent-up heat immediately. After rolling down the windows, I bent forward to put my key into the ignition.

"This heat is really miserable," I thought, and my discomfort seemed to quash the joy and the peace of the last several hours. My doubts returned. "What's happening here?" I asked myself querulously. "How could I feel so close to someone I just met? Maybe I'm wrong. Maybe I misjudged the whole thing."

Voicing a quiet plea for help, I turned on the engine. The first spatters of rain hit the windshield. I grimly rolled the windows back up, suddenly furious at myself. "Oh, great," I said angrily, "*Wet* heat."

Several months earlier, I had noticed that the car's heating system would not work. I had fiddled with the buttons to no avail. Instead of a welcoming warmth, there was only a dark, unlit dashboard. I knew little about the car's electrical system and resolved to drive over to my neighborhood service station later that afternoon. It had been a mild winter and wasn't terribly cold anyway, I reasoned.

But I procrastinated about having the heater fixed that day and in the following week. Later, when I needed gas, I asked the station attendant to check out the problem. He probed about, ruffling his hair and shaking his head. He finally emerged from the interior of the car, a small wired device in his palm.

"Here it is," he grinned. "Your electrical system is blown. You'll have to take it back in to the dealer. He'll replace it for you."

I thanked him and drove away, disappointed. Now I'd have to rent a car and go through the logistics involved with having a car in the shop. I promised myself to take care of it "one of these days." The weather remained mild and I didn't really need either heat or air conditioning. I missed the lighted dash, with its mileage and fuel indicators, but I learned to get along without it.

Now it was late May. Uncomfortably warm days had arrived, and I was scheduled in a few days to take the car in to the dealer to get it fixed.

So here I sat, frustrated and miserably hot in front of the house on Christy Lane. I need a miracle, I thought. Somehow the doubts about my Christy compulsion and the physical discomfort of the heat were mixed up together. Thunder cracked and lightning streaked across a darkening sky. Where was all the love and energy I felt earlier? I wondered. And what is this thing called energy *about*? Sighing, I pulled the car from the curb and drove down the street.

A few moments later, I felt something brush across my feet. Startled, I looked down and saw nothing. The sensation continued. Then I realized it was air, flowing from somewhere, hot air. The windows were closed. Still, heat was pouring into the car.

I pulled over to the curb. Suddenly, the dashboard lit up, the digits glowing green and alive. I punched the heat buttons to "off" and the cold ones to "on." Cool air wafted out. Every vent gave forth the miracle of air-conditioning.

I couldn't believe what had happened. Everything was working! I drove home in amazement and awe, yet also expecting the lights to go out at any minute. God, or Grace, or the Power of Love had appeared in unmistakable form. The car performed to perfection, never losing energy nor intensity.

I canceled the impending appointment at the dealership and weeks later, I drove in for a regular automotive checkup. I explained what had happened to an unbelieving serviceman.

"No way that could happen," he flatly stated.

"Well, see for yourself," I smiled confidently, starting the engine. The dashboard glowed. He fished out the panel and stared at it in disbelief. "This is burned out. I don't understand it."

"Neither do I," I replied, "but I'll accept the miracle anyway."

"Well, sure," he stammered, at a loss for words. "I'll finish checking out your car."

I thought back to the afternoon of the first visit with Tarran. I remembered the wonder and the joy that came with the "miracle of the car." The same tiny jolts of fear I had known on other occasions of a miraculous nature shot through me. But this time was different. I now had a friend to share my questions and astonishment with, someone who understood.

Shortly afterward I stopped by the Biblical Arts Center one afternoon on my regular round of errands. *The Christ* had been exhibited for almost three years by then. When I visited it, I always paused to view the huge Nativity painting on the wall, which led into the current exhibit room. I found myself continually inspired by its tender beauty, and I often wondered where Christy had found his Mary. Her young face was delicate, touchingly naive, yet her eyes spoke of confidence, and her whole attitude was one of faith. She had fulfilled her purpose, and she knew it.

I visited the center's new exhibit and, as always, turned down the hall to spend a few minutes with *The Christ*. Another painting was hanging in its place! I was shocked and turned to see if it had been moved to a different wall. It was not there.

A surge of disappointment rushed through me. I felt alone, abandoned. I could feel tears welling in my eyes. Immediately I asked the curator what had happened to the painting. He told me it had been requested back in Nashville. Word of the painting had spread, and others elsewhere wanted to see it. It had been crated for shipment several days earlier and had left the museum the day before. Why had no one told me? I left in a fog of distress.

I had not realized how deeply attached to Christy's work I had become. I felt that I had lost a part of myself, and I grieved for it. While being glad that others would have the opportunity to see the painting, I still missed terribly the face I had come to love so deeply. Many times I had felt that face respond to me in love also.

I surmised that this quest had ended, yet it felt unfinished. The painting and the Christy Quest had become a symbol of hope during a time of pain. I had moved on. So had *The Christ*. There were others who needed its special grace.

Still, this knowledge didn't satisfy me. Fortunately, the next step in the quest was not far away.

Out of the blue a Dallas friend, Carleen Smith, suggested I accompany her to New York City for a gift trade show. I readily agreed. My first thought was "The Hotel des Artistes!"

I looked up at the carved gargoyles adorning the facade of the Hotel. Their strange, grinning faces added to the magic of the moment. We stood at the front door, pausing to notice the inscribed "#1." A spacious tiled entry offered access to the Café off to the right side and led up several steps to the Hotel lobby, straight ahead.

The Hotel des Artistes

I was finally in Christy territory. The sense of adventure, of anticipation, was powerful. I was in the very spot Christopher Burge had told me about at that long-ago dinner party. I wandered through the lobby, touching the few chairs and sofas scattered about. The elevators were age-worn and elegant. I saw an ancient telephone switchboard in a tiny cubbyhole office and a larger office where an elderly gentleman sat behind a huge desk. Another small room beckoned from across the way—musty, dusty, crammed with old books and memorabilia.

I yearned to explore whatever lay inside. The setting, once the scene played out by Christy and his entourage, filled me with excitement. Carleen broke into my reverie, urging that we hurry into the Café. Reluctantly I turned, following her to the restaurant door.

There was a large crowd inside, some standing in line, some moving toward tables. An attractive young woman stood behind the reservations desk marking off names on a very long list. My heart sank, and the feeling was confirmed when she smilingly shook her head "no." There was no way we could be seated for lunch. She explained that reservations were made weeks, even months in advance.

I pleaded that we had only one day here. Could we at least walk through the Café, as I longed to see the Christy murals. She smiled again, saying "Of course—and if you're lucky, you might find a place to sit at the bar, toward the back."

A few minutes later Carleen was again tugging at me. I couldn't understand her impatience. I wanted to stand rooted, gazing at the glorious nudes rollicking over the walls. One more jerk forward from her and I mutely followed. The place was all I had expected in beauty and charm and warmth, but I had not anticipated the immediacy, the electricity of the place. The figures on the wall came alive somehow, blending into and among the diners. One such luncheon guest seated herself at a tiny table next to the end of the bar. Carleen and I were fortunate to grab two seats at the same end of the bar, sighing in relief as we pulled ourselves up onto the barstools. The dark-haired woman turned to face us, and I saw why Carleen had been so insistent. It was Jacqueline Kennedy Onassis.

A handsome young bartender nodded to take our order. We asked his advice, and he immediately replied, "The Ilona Torte, the wickedest dessert in New York City." It was chocolate, of course. Sensing our unfamiliarity with the Café, he offered as much information as possible between serving others and polishing the gleaming bar surface. From a cabinet he brought forth a cookbook which, he explained, would give a brief history of the place. Christy's nudes decorated the cover.

I glanced to the wall, a bit to the left of us. There, gazing out from a simple frame was a drawing, a sketch of the artist himself. It was the first time I had seen a picture of him. His friend and fellow artist, James Montgomery Flagg, had drawn it. I was looking directly into a mischievous countenance. There was a conspiratorial wink, as if expressing a shared secret. He seemed to say, "Welcome!"

From my daydream I heard someone whisper, "Look, there's Bernadette Peters." She was sitting directly below Christy's portrait. Billows of curls framed her face. Her eyes were expressive and large. She spoke with animation to the two men with her, gesturing with her hands. She was the perfect image of the Christy Girl.

We stayed in the Café for two hours. The crowd finally thinned, providing us the chance to wander more freely in and around the tables. I scanned each mural and each photograph, as though committing them to memory. I didn't know when or if I would be there again.

The Christy Quest lay dormant again for a while after I got back home. I was still studying the *Course in Miracles* on my own. About a year after the New York trip, I heard about a *Miracles* study group that met on Sunday mornings. A remarkable young man named Curt led the discussions. Years of intense study of the *Course* and the joyful warmth of his nature made his lectures powerful.

I asked Curt if he knew that the painting on the cover of Ken Wapnick's *Forgiveness and Jesus* had been found. He replied that he hadn't known. Then he said, "There is another painting."

"What do you mean?" I asked.

"There was," Curt continued, "a Christy painting, Christ rising above a battlefield. It was on St. Simon's Island, Georgia, the last I knew." He offered to send me a postcard of it, and I eagerly accepted the offer. It arrived in the mail a few days later.

As soon as I saw the painting, I could feel its power. It was titled *Christ after Chaos – the Prince of Peace.* I wanted to see it in person.

St. Simon's Island is directly off the coast of Georgia. I called the Wesley Conference Center on the island for information and was sent a museum brochure which told briefly of the painting. I was intrigued by the locale. The Wesley brothers, John and Charles, had landed on the site in 1735 after sailing to America from their home in England. Thus, St. Simon's Island became the first location in which Methodism was preached in the United States. I wondered how and why Christy's painting had come to this historic setting.

I already felt a connection with the Methodist Center. After my father died in 1979, my mother married a retired Methodist minister, Dr. Herbert T. Minga. Herb was a grand person, a man who loved his work, his congregations, every individual he met, and my mother. He had been a family pastor, a true shepherd of his flock. "Bless your heart" was his lifelong motto. My mother and he had eight happy and active years together before Herb's death in 1988. As a Minister Emeritus, Herb continued his work with baptisms, weddings, funerals, visitations of the ill, and occasional sermons. Herb held a deep affection for the Methodist Church. For me, knowing this kind man was like a return to the faith of my childhood, a "coming home" to that part of my life.

Because I was feeling so drawn to Georgia, my friend David and I decided to tour the southern coastal states in the summer of 1991. We wanted to see as many Christy paintings as we could.

The "Deep South" is famous for its Civil War history, its slower pace of life, molasses accents, magnolias, red earth, hush puppies, and Stephen Foster songs. Stephen Foster Park at White Springs, Florida, close to the Georgia state line, is off the beaten track. I knew Christy paintings were there. David, a skilled map-interpreter, had to search longer than usual to find it. At last country back roads led us to the entrance. At mid-morning it was already hot. The Suwannee River ran lazily through the magnolias, elms, and oaks. Heavy gray Spanish moss hung from spreading boughs. On the hour, Foster melodies chimed.

As we walked across the almost-deserted parking lot, the heat rose in humid waves off the gravel and concrete walkways. We spotted the gift shop and headed toward the guide behind the counter. The Christy paintings were in another building, she informed us, and showed us prints of both works.

Another guide met us in the foyer of the large building where Christy's paintings hung. *Beautiful Dreamer* and *Many Happy Days I Squandered* were displayed on huge walls, across from each other, in an equally massive room. Foster's small piano stood in the center of the area, with museum cases on each side.

Christy portrayed Stephen Foster as a youth, a young girl playmate by his side, surrounded by blooming trees and fluttering birds, in the *Many Happy Days* painting. A small boat waits on the river below. Christy, I remembered, had described his own childhood as idyllic. The faces of these children reflected the joy and freedom of youth, yet there seemed to be a sense of poignancy, as well. The portrait of Foster as a maturing composer was circled by visions of beautiful Southern belles, his imagination captured by their charm.

The *Beautiful Dreame*r lies back upon a green meadow, one length of her gossamer wrap falling into Foster's raised right hand. It is a romantic painting, encompassing Foster's love of music, women, nature, and an inbred Southern sensitivity. Christy and Foster, I thought, a comradeship of feeling and of creativity, the blending of artist and subject.

"Christy did another Stephen Foster painting," the guide called after us as we were leaving the room. "I believe it is somewhere in Kentucky." I made a mental note.

The Methodist Conference Center on St. Simon's Island is situated on an arm of land overlooking the ocean. Giant oaks, laced with Spanish moss, dot the area. On a beautiful Georgia morning, warm and clear-skied, we drove through iron gates which announced the Wesleyan heritage. There are two chapels. One is the classic picture of white clapboard with a tall belled steeple; the other is a small stone edifice poised over the water's edge.

We parked and walked toward the museum. Few cars or people disturbed the serene grounds. Birds darted about singing and swooping, squirrels paused to eye us with curiosity. The chapel bells rang out the hour, 10 A.M. We entered the building, where a large statue of Charles Wesley stood in the central rotunda. Striking portraits of the twelve disciples of Christ were exhibited along the left wall.

Lucy Clary, whom I had contacted earlier, came to greet us in the lobby. We accompanied her down a long hall to view *The Prince of Peace.*

"It needs to be framed," Lucy said. "We removed the canvas to have it cleaned and haven't replaced the old frame."

"Well, framed or not," I said, "it is magnificent."

Shafts of light from a side window filtered across Christy's work. "It's the same face," David quietly stated, "the same as in the portrait of Christ."

I nodded, agreeing. "It is much more evident in the actual painting than in the postcard picture."

I continued to study the work while Lucy told us its history. The museum was dedicated to Bishop Arthur C. Moore, who was bishop more than fifty years ago. Bishop Moore's central office was in the Methodist Church's Manhattan headquarters. He had commissioned Christy to produce the "Peace" painting in 1942. Its official title became *The Coming Peace and the Prince of Peace.* The painting remained in Bishop Moore's office for twenty years. At the time of his retirement, it was presented to him. He chose to bring it to the museum here at Epworth-by-the-Sea.

It was also mass-produced as a poster. In 1943 the Methodist Church began a campaign called "A Crusade for a New World Order" to promote world peace. Christy's poster was chosen as its visual symbol. The posters were sent to the 42,000 Methodist congregations throughout America for prominent display. Mass meetings were held in more than one hundred U.S. cities from coast to coast. At each meeting, everyone present was given a postcard reproduction of the Christy work. During these sessions, Methodists addressed these cards to members of the armed forces, stating their belief in the necessity for a spiritual emphasis at each peace table conference. The crusade's slogan was formed: "That Peace May Be Won With A One-Cent Stamp."

The painting was given a special berth on the Freedom Train, which traveled through America during the 1940s. I found it interesting that Christy-the-patriot, who had called so many youths into military service during both World Wars via his numerous posters, had become Christy-the-peacemaker in the last decade of his life.

Once again, I heard the words, "There's another painting." I turned from my reverie before *The Prince of Peace*. Lucy had called the Methodist Conference Center in Lake Junaluska, North Carolina. They confirmed her question about another religious painting by Christy, answering that they also owned one. It was entitled *The Christ Commission* and was housed in the Chapel of Peace on their grounds.

As we left, I strongly sensed Herb's presence. "Bless your heart" were the unmistakable words which rang in my mind as we drove back through the iron gates.

4

Christy grew up in Ohio, so it was natural that I wanted to explore his territory there, which was just south of Zanesville on the Muskingum River near Duncan Falls. He returned to his boyhood home in 1908 from New York, rebuilt it and named it The Barracks. The name was in honor of his experience in the Spanish-American War, when he served as a war correspondent and artist with Teddy Roosevelt's Rough Riders in Cuba.

Christy found refuge in his boyhood home at a period when his first marriage was disintegrating and he was struggling with alcoholism and depression. He moved back to New York in 1915, not long after his divorce from Maybelle Thompson was final.

Carol Ann Kendrick, a long-time Dallas friend who would become my questing partner, and I decided upon a departure date in the summer of 1991. I made some preliminary telephone calls to Ohioans I hoped to meet. My list began with Norris Schneider, who had written a pamphlet about Christy's life and who then, at ninety-three, lived in Zanesville. I also wanted to visit the Ohio Historical Society and the governor's mansion in Columbus.

Just before we left, I called Melinda Knapp at the Society and learned that she'd found several Christy paintings in their collection. Two were portraits of a beautiful woman named Elise Ford. One of these was *The Summit,* then hanging in the governor's mansion. It included the woman's young daughter. The other, called *My Sidekick,* was displayed in the Society's museum. The title of the painting intrigued me immediately, as well as the inevitable question of "Who is she?"

Over the next few days I mused about this mystery woman. It seemed unusual to me that Christy had painted her twice. She must have been more important to him than the usual stream of portrait clients who appeared on his canvases. And there was the enigmatic title, *My Sidekick.* The delicious sense of "this is important" reappeared and remained.

In mid-July we left Dallas and headed northeast. When we drove into Columbus around midnight, it was raining heavily. We were tired, cross from the constant deluge which had held us up the entire day, and anxious to find our hotel in the labyrinth of unfamiliar downtown streets.

The next morning, rested and much calmer, I munched on a muffin and sipped coffee in our room, as I unearthed my telephone list. My first call was to Melinda to confirm our appointment for the following morning.

She responded with obvious excitement in her voice, "Helen, I've been waiting for your call. Something very interesting has happened."

"What is it?" I asked, my own excitement matching hers.

"Call Bobbie Wiard at the governor's mansion right away. Then call me back," she added mysteriously.

I immediately dialed the governor's mansion, and after a few moments, Bobbie's pleasant voice answered. "Good morning and welcome to Ohio. I have news for you." Curiosity was churning within me, and I waited to hear more.

"Have you talked with Melinda yet?" Bobbie asked.

"She told me to call *you.*"

"Well," Bobbie's voice became very quiet. "You won't believe this, but the woman in the Elise painting was here the day before yesterday."

I was astonished. "You mean that Elise herself was here?" I asked.

"No, Elise died some years ago, but her daughter came to see the painting. She was here for only one day, and has gone back to her home in Lafayette, Indiana."

How I had yearned to meet someone, anyone, who had actually posed for Christy! Now someone had appeared, and I had missed her by a mere forty-eight hours. "Tell me all about her," I said.

"Well, the amazing thing is— " she paused, "she's the daughter of Elise Ford *and* Howard Chandler Christy."

I blinked. Bobbie continued, caught up in the excitement of the revelation. "Her name is Holly Longuski. Her husband came with her. They, like you, had been hoping to get to Columbus for a long time and kept having setbacks. This particular day unexpectedly opened up for them, so they drove over from Indiana. I told her about your interest in Christy, and she wants to talk with you."

It was an incredible piece of luck. Carol Ann, at work on a piece of needlepoint across the room, looked up in surprise. "What, what, what?" she wanted to know.

"His daughter, Christy's daughter, was here," I mouthed back to her startled look.

The next morning was oppressively hot, misty and overcast. Right on time we pulled up to the large red-brick building boasting the Ohio Historical Society's name and emblem. Set in gentle hills, its site complemented by green lawns, the building seemed to welcome us up its broad steps and into the entrance.

"Melinda, we're here!" I sang out over the telephone at the reception desk.

Vast marbled areas, display cases, and various artifacts of Ohio's heritage dotted the walls on the way to Melinda's office.

A young brunette in a stylish beige sportsuit greeted us. "Let's go." Melinda grinned. "First, we'll look at the *Sidekick* painting and then we'll drive over to the warehouse for a trip through the archives."

"Great," I answered, already moving toward the door. "I can't wait to see Elise."

"I can imagine how excited you must be hearing about Holly's visit." Melinda spoke as we walked.

"Tell me about her." I was aflame with curiosity.

"She was charming," Melinda continued, "and as an adult, her face still looks just like it did as a child. Huge brown eyes and dark hair. She was thrilled to be here, and her husband was, too. He had never seen either of the Elise portraits."

We had arrived back downstairs. Melinda led us to a wall hung with several paintings. Suddenly, we stood before Elise. It was *My Sidekick*.

"Elise herself sent this to us along with *The Summit*."

I studied the model whom Christy had affectionately and intimately termed his "sidekick." A pale green satin gown clung provocatively to her youthful body. The fabric afforded a slight glimpse of seductive curves beneath. She was posed on a bench or chair, a black stole draped over one graceful hand, in front of what must have been a tapestry.

The muted, woven figures behind her suggested a religious work of art. "She looks like an angel," I heard myself saying. "She fits right into the setting." The heavy black and gold embossed frame had been expertly chosen and added to the medieval feeling in the painting. Elise seemed familiar. I thought that I had seen her face not once, but many times before.

As we walked away from the portrait, I knew that the lovely face of Christy's model would linger in my mind for a long time. I would not forget her. "Keep searching. There is so much to discover. I want my story told." Were those her words, or mine?

We piled into our car for the ride to the Historical Society's warehouse. The building, which housed Ohio's prized artifacts and paintings, was some miles away. Kim Feinknopf was the archival curator there.

Once inside the corrugated metal warehouse, we located Kim.

"We have only two Christy works," she said, "and they've been pulled out, waiting for you."

We followed her out of the central office and into a huge area packed with shelves. "There must be thousands of canvases stored in here," I marveled.

"You're right," answered Melinda, expertly threading her way among wooden crates and cardboard packing cases.

"Here we are," announced Kim, "and here are the Christy

My Sidekick

pieces." She pointed to a large sepia-toned work which stood against tall shelves. "This was probably a preliminary drawing or layout, a study, before he painted the actual work in oils."

Although roughly laid out, the monotone sketch was unmistakably Christy. Several American Indian figures were represented, along with a deer-skinned frontiersman and, of course, the inevitable damsel.

"This has to have been an illustration for one of his books," Carol Ann said.

"Maybe so," Kim answered. "We're not certain; we know it is an early work."

"Here's a very early sketch," said Melinda, drawing our attention to a small, simply framed drawing which lay on a worktable. We circled the table, peering closely at the dim and torn sketch. The smudged date read 1887.

"He was only fourteen years old then," I mused.

"This piece was found hanging in one of the Ohio Historical Society sites in another part of the state," Kim explained. "I believe it was in a farmhouse."

"You're right," Melinda added. "The state decided to restore the place and removed the furniture, sending it all here until the project was completed."

"It came here at a perfect time as far as I'm concerned," I said. "What a treat to see something he produced as a boy."

I thought of "Smiley" Christy, his good-natured grin providing the youthful nickname. "All he really wanted to do was paint," I remembered. "School went by the wayside and stayed there."

Our next step was to look at Norris Schneider's research material in the Society's library. In 1975, as a high school teacher, he wrote a short newspaper article on Christy. It was later published as a monograph. Until the advent of Susan Meyer's now-classic *America's Great Illustrators* in 1978, Schneider's pamphlet provided the only available history of Christy's personal life.

Ohio's land, legends, and people infuse Schneider's work, both as a historian and as a teacher. He painstakingly followed the Christy career, personal and public, over a long lifetime, meticulously gathering data, clipping articles from magazines, journals, and newspapers, and finally, creating scrapbooks to hold his voluminous research.

After lunch, we wound our way through halls and museum byways, ending up at the glass doors marked research library. When the scrapbooks we requested arrived at our table, I opened the largest. After a few minutes of turning pages, I realized the enormity of the task. After an hour, my mind was blurred with confusion and my vision with tiny dancing black squiggles.

An hour later, I was aching from head to toe with cramped muscles and frustration. Schneider's personal correspondence, art exhibit and gallery programs, invitations to private and media events, genealogical information, and a few Christy family letters and transcribed telephone conversations were there.

Schneider wrote with a wry pen, noting the artist's bent toward scandal as well as creativity. Christy's infamous "frontier spirit" was as compelling to Schneider as his artistic renown.

I gave up, shut the heavy scrapbook, and headed for a breath of air. I found Carol Ann in the same condition, leaning against the stone steps outside the museum. "I can't decide which pages to copy, which articles I already have, which are too dim to photograph, *anything*," I groaned.

I decided to have the entire scrapbook photocopied. I would read it at home. At five o'clock we gathered up our cameras and bags, then stopped by Elise's portrait for one last look before plodding out to the parking lot.

"So much information," I sighed. "I feel overwhelmed."

That night the TV hummed and sputtered, ignored. Visions of newspaper and magazine clip-outs, letters to be deciphered, faded photos, and Norris' handwritten notes appeared in jumbled chaos as I slept. But when I awoke the next morning, it was the intriguing face of Elise Ford which signalled the beginning of a new day.

Through the rain we drove away from the city into the residential suburb of Bexley. Huge trees shaded and enhanced the beautiful homes which we passed on our route to Parkview Avenue. We found the Tudor governor's mansion easily on a large corner lot. Its gabled roof was slate-covered. Exposed wooden beams criss-crossed its stone-work facade.

"What a wonderful place," I said to Carol Ann. "Imposing, yet as warm as a real home." We parked on the side street a few steps from the back door. Uniformed guards appeared, waving us with friendly grins to "go right in." Carol Ann and I stood for a moment at the back door, bags and cameras in hand, and umbrellas dripping. Then Bobbie opened it with a bright smile of welcome.

"Come in. Come in out of the rain!" She was tiny, almost fragile, with an air of quiet efficiency.

We followed her down a hall, off of which an inviting kitchen beckoned. Children's bright drawings were displayed on the walls, along with a bulletin board filled with family pictures and more formal gubernatorial awards.

Bobbie led us into a spacious entry area flanked by a magnificent staircase. Her brown eyes glowed as she told us of Holly's visit earlier.

While we talked, we walked over to the foot of the massive staircase. Several steps above us were the faces of Elise and Holly. The portrait was huge, ideal in proportion to the soaring wall where it hung. "Holly told us that she was five or six years old at the time, and she did *not* like sitting still, posing, for so long," Bobbie said.

I gazed at these surprising new characters in the Christy script. Elise was exquisite, glowing, a woman who was deeply loved and knew it. The artist had masterfully captured her radiant identity. He had brought her to life—or rather his love for her, an unmistakable statement in brush-stroked clarity. The serenity of her gaze and the grace of her posed figure indicated that she loved the man who painted her. All I wanted to do was to stand there absorbing the painting.

"Holly was easily recognizable," Bobbie was saying. "She still looks like she did then, with her long, dark brown hair and big brown eyes. She is also an artist."

I tried to see the adult Holly, but all I could see was a little girl clutching a worn picture book, a discarded pink satin bonnet at her feet. Christy had painted his young daughter with tenderness and pride in her beauty. She mirrored her mother's exquisite dark coloring and facial bone structure.

I heard approaching footsteps and glanced down the several stairs to the foyer. Governor and Mrs. Voinovich walked into the entry accompanied by a guest. They bade him goodbye and turned with a gracious "hello" for Carol Ann and me. I was too wrapped into Christy's painting to pursue a conversation. They headed toward the back hall with a wink and a wave.

The next day we were off to the Ohio countryside. We hoped to find Norris Schneider. When I'd called Norris the previous summer, he'd had difficulty hearing me, but we managed a conversation as best we could. He gave me verbal snapshots of Christy: meandering daily through Central Park accompanied by his flask ("just in case of snake bite"); wild courtroom battles during his divorce from Maybelle; and views of The Barracks. His wife had recently died, he said, and he was lonely. I called him again just before we left on this trip, and he told me he had moved to a smaller place, an apartment. Yes, he'd be glad to see us.

The day was sunny and quite warm. Zanesville is on the Muskingum River. I remembered Christy's fascination with the lumbering steamboats, plowing back and forth, on "his" river. He rode on them, swam around them, and, later, was often carried to them after a night of carousing in the local bars.

The retirement home where Norris lived was close by, in a tree-shaded neighborhood. I inquired at the desk for Mr. Schneider. No one there by that name. My heart sank, and I asked an aide if Norris could be anywhere else.

He said, "Sure. I'll bet he's over in the other building," and pointed it out to us. My heart rose.

When Norris answered my knock, he was puzzled by who we were. Perhaps he didn't believe I'd really come. After a moment, he said, "Well, we could visit at lunch. You come with me." He reached for a cane and off we went.

The lunchroom was already filling up, but we found a table. I asked if I might use my tape recorder and Norris nodded. I didn't learn anything new, but I felt that I was fulfilling a pledge made in the quiet of my heart. At least he knew that his work was appreciated.

After leaving Norris, we drove to downtown Zanesville. Spying an antique mall sign, we parked and went inside. "No Christys here," we were politely informed and directed to another shop down the street. Here, luck was in our favor. We met a husband and wife who led us to several wonderful old framed prints and added a further piece of information. An acquaintance owned Christy's desk. They were sure there were Christy papers in the drawers.

We made one further stop, after a few wrong turns, at a real estate agency. The agent we were in search of, who owned some Christy pieces, was also absent. The time was passing too quickly, and we still had the Duncan Falls stop on our schedule. We said goodbye to Zanesville and, finding the highway, pointed the car south.

As we drove toward Duncan Falls I wavered between happiness at finally getting there and fear of not finding The Barracks. The highway ran through the center of the small town. It was garage-sale Saturday. All the neighbors were out and browsing in each other's for-sale offerings. The church and the few stores were decorated with bargains and banners. A flag waved.

I took a snapshot and thought of Christy's patriotic spirit. He boomed the old cannon every July 4 and ran the flag up and down each morning and evening. His colorful posters exhorted enlistment in the armed forces: "If I were a man, I'd join the Navy!" Thousands of young men answered the call of this Christy Girl. Later, civilians were urged to support "our fighting boys" with Christy posters.

Would anyone remember him?

Almost out of gas, we found a station. Several cars were ahead of us at the pumps. I hopped out, hoping the teenaged cashier might have a history-minded, story-telling grandparent. He had never heard of Christy. "Did he play a banjo?" he asked.

A customer from the car just ahead of ours overheard me. She said, "You might ask Ruth Baker over at the grocery. She's lived here forever and knows a lot."

We went across the highway to a little store filled with food and fishing gear. A plump, smiling woman stood chatting behind the counter—Ruthie. "Can I help you?" she asked.

I asked for Christy information. She beamed and replied, "Sure! Wait a minute and we'll talk."

When Ruthie finished at the cash register she briskly led me out the old screen door and across the street. We were going to visit Hilda Pagel. Hilda was easy to find. She was spading a plot of vegetables outside her small frame house. When she looked up from her work, I saw a remarkable face. Would that Christy had captured her, I thought. Her hair was long and thick, gray, framing a face that must have laughed a lot.

Dressed in old denim, she extended a dirty, work-hardened hand. Oh yes, she remembered the artist well. And her father, she proudly added, had done carpentry work and posed for him. She seemed lost in thought for a moment, then leaned the spade against a rough wooden fence and hustled into her house. Back she came, bearing a photograph in a dusty frame. A newspaper candid shot of Christy's last visit here. His wife, Nancy, was beside him.

Ruthie gave us instructions on how to find The Barracks. "It's hard to see. You have to look for a stop sign and turn left and go real slow up a hill, winding, but don't give up. You'll see it."

I reluctantly said goodbye, hugged Ruthie, and blew a kiss to Hilda, thanking them for their guidance.

We drove down the highway, pointing the car toward the turnoff. We missed it the first time. On the second try we found it. Ruthie was right. It was a tough way up, a tree-shadowed, overgrown route.

I rolled down the window. There was a hush, except for the singing of birds and the crunch of rocks below the tires. On and on we went, carefully climbing, twisting and turning, and then, as quickly as we'd entered the darkness of the trees, we were out of them and sunshine flooded the road. Up ahead lay a stone building, hazy, almost shimmering in the heat. As we drew closer, a dog began to bark, announcing our presence.

Christy loved animals. He always had pets as a boy. His first painting was of a black and white cow—a wooden sign unmistakenly stating "Butcher Shop." His Great Dane, Sargent, was named after his idol, the famed American portraitist, John Singer Sargent.

There was no Great Dane here today, but rather a black, curly wriggling mass of cocker spaniel. We parked on a gravel drive. I leaped out. Carol Ann was a bit more cautious. I looked around, saw a huge old paint-peeled red barn, several other smaller buildings, and a flagpole.

The porch door opened, another dog came bounding out, and a youngish woman dressed in shorts and a tank top emerged. She introduced herself—Barb Hayes. I apologized for the lack of a call beforehand and explained why we were there. Barb relaxed and invited us inside. Scattered toys on the crowded porch spoke of children. The dogs frisked and ran circles around our feet, then comradely followed us in. The kitchen was obviously a center of activity, the linoleum tired and worn. On a wall leading into the dining area, Carol Ann pointed to a framed Christy print. It was *The Christ*.

How long had it been there? Barb began to open drawers, searching out old scrapbooks. She pulled out pictures and letters. I was enthralled, every pore open to absorb the "he-lived-here" energy. We saw other old prints, early illustrations from books, hanging on the faded walls.

Barb had been preparing for a nursing exam, studying that afternoon before her children came in from school. Her husband Tom was the son of the family that had bought the land many years before.

Several destructive fires had wiped out the "big" house and damaged this smaller one also. The farm had once been a family compound, as well as a retreat for friends, townspeople, and models. Christy's parents died here, as did his sister Rose. Christy stored many of his illustrations here after he moved back to New York. Later, he called and ordered them burned. He wanted to be known as a serious artist, not an illustrator.

Barb had her hands full, taking care of her family, the old home, and her school work. I could feel that she was tired, even overwhelmed. As she searched for Christy material, and Carol Ann browsed with her, I walked through the house. A large living area boasted a big fireplace. Another small den-like room led off it. Several Christy posters, reminders of the past, adorned the walls. The place was rundown—threadbare—but the bare bones of old beauty, of old times and the romance of the past still lingered.

I stood by the fireplace, lost in thought. I could picture the evenings here: Christy sitting in contemplation of the canvas-of-the-day, pipe smoke curling. If there were guests—and his memoirs indicate many of them—there would be shared stories, memories, laughter. Rich and poor, the famous and ordinary folk were his friends. He drew people to him with his charisma. And I, too, had been pulled to this room.

Carol Ann called out, "Come and look at this!" There was a bill of sale with Christy's unmistakable signature; Christmas cards ("Greetings from Howard & Nancy," the Biblical Arts Nativity pictured on one); other notes, jotted scribbles; the written paraphernalia of life. I pored over them, hoping to glimpse more of the artist's persona.

Later, Barb and I, accompanied by the dogs, walked outside to explore the spacious grounds. As we wandered, she spoke of her feelings about the place. Her childhood years had been in an urban area without the close presence of birds, flowers, trees, and all the green gifts a country home offered. She loved the freedom of space, of the outside world. The seasonal changes fascinated her.

We strolled slowly, breathing in the fresh air. Barb, shyly at first, began to share her dream. Her hope was to restore the place as it was in 1908. Sadly, there was no money to do so. At least I could affirm her vision. I, too, had a dream—of bringing forth a book. We were puzzle pieces, Barb and I, in a giant jigsaw. The complete picture we might not see, yet we could pledge to continue to believe in it.

We stood looking at a small structure, a guest house, its walls almost destroyed by time, weather, and lack of upkeep. Yet still it stood, however off-center and crooked. I looked up toward the roof where, surprisingly, a bright blue porcelain cat arched its back and seemed to hiss a warning to the dogs below. I peeked into a tiny room. It must have made a delightful playhouse for children. The wind sang through the tall trees.

A battered old red barn rose three stories. A family van was parked at the front of a large ramp leading into the ground floor. Barb signalled me to follow her inside.

The main room was huge, cavernous, dark with shadows but spiked by shafts of light piercing through the wooden slats. Startled pigeons flew from their nests among the beams. Machinery dozed in rusty piles. The trappings of farm animals lay about. The dogs sniffed and explored. In spite of its vastness, there was a sense of warmth and coziness in the room.

Steps off to the left led up to the next level, and we carefully squeezed our way between cobwebs and debris. The second floor was divided into two areas. Sunshine poured through a large window opening on the left side. Perfect northern light streamed in—nature floodlighting the place. It had once been a magnificent studio, a work of art itself.

Christy must have painted away the daylight hours in this room, oblivious to the outside world. I knew, in that moment, the same feeling of absorption. Barb pointed to the far wall. Mementos, toys, and boxes were stacked against it. Underneath a tip of blue winked out—the models' platform, on rollers. Webbed cross-country skis were crossed and hung on the wall above.

There was so much of life here, of yesterday blending into this moment, of the magic of now intertwined with the magic of then. Barb told me of the parties held on the lawns, the games played. There had been tennis courts. Carriages and wagons filled with friends and visitors came clopping up the hill, the guests arrayed in swimming suits or costumed for dining.

From below I heard a car honk. I walked to the window and looked down at Carol Ann. She waved, indicating it was time to go. I knew she was right. We had stayed a long time for an unexpected visit. As though emerging from a time tunnel, I slowly headed for the stairs.

5

Saturday morning after breakfast Carol Ann reached for her needlepoint, and I reached for the telephone. I was nervous. At last I would make contact with Christy's daughter.

A recorded voice clicked on, "The number you have dialed is not a working number. Please hang up and dial again." I did and this time, the line was busy. I took a sip of coffee, paced the room for a while, and called again.

The phone rang repeatedly. Finally, "Hello?" a female voice questioned.

"Holly?"

"Yes, this is Holly," came the answer. "Is this Helen?"

"Yes, it's me," I said, surprised. "Calling from Ohio."

"I've been waiting and hoping for your call," she burst in. "I have so much to tell you and so much to ask."

We talked for an hour—a lifetime, it seemed, to be thimbled into one conversation. "I wish we could visit in person," I said wistfully.

"So do I!" said Holly emphatically. "Please come. Jim and I would love to have you here."

"How about it?" I whispered to Carol Ann. She shrugged, "I guess so. Why not?" She got up and began rummaging for a map.

"We could leave in the morning and be there by late afternoon,"

I said. Carol Ann unearthed our well-used U.S. map, pointing out the distance involved while I scribbled the directions. When I hung up, I turned to Carol Ann.

"Well, Don Quixote," she said, her eyes alight with amusement, "it seems that we're off to find the windmills of Indiana."

The next morning I paced around the front entry of our hotel, waiting impatiently while the doorman retrieved our car from the parking garage. "You'll be worn out before we start," Carol Ann stated wryly.

When the car arrived, Carol Ann as usual took the wheel, and I arranged myself among the paraphernalia. It was a gray day, the sky ominous with dark clouds. A soft mist fell.

"More rain," Carol Ann observed.

"Who cares?" I responded. "We're adventuring. That's the important thing."

"Okay, Quixote, get out the map. Our adventure needs some road signs."

Dutifully, I obeyed, spreading open the creased map. There it was: the highway, bright red and clear in its direction. This was the magic time, the beginning. The road lay before us and with it the delicious anticipation of we-knew-not-what-to-come.

The day turned sunny. We ignored the tempting antique shops and roadside eateries along the route. I pulled out the notes I'd made while talking to Holly, bits and pieces, scattered and sketchy, of a fascinating personal history. She had longed, as had I, to meet someone who was interested in her artist-father.

It was almost 6 P.M. before we wheeled up in front of our motel near the Purdue University area where Holly and Jim lived. We hurriedly threw our bags inside the room, did a quick wash-up, and then I reached for the phone.

Holly answered immediately, "Where are you?" More directions were given.

"We're about fifteen minutes from their house," I explained to Carol Ann, my hand cupping the receiver.

"Well, don't start another conversation. Just say good-bye, and let's go," cautioned Carol Ann, knowing my inclination to talk on and on.

A few minutes later we were back in the car with a city map

unfurled between us. After a few false turns, we followed a "Purdue University This Way" sign.

We entered a tree-lined residential area and circled the nearest blocks several times, searching out address numbers and Holly's guidepost descriptions ("Just past the corner drugstore." "Two stop signs in succession." "Our house looks like a mini-castle.")—and we were there.

The Longuski home indeed resembled a small beamed and timbered castle with cut-glass windows, a big wooden front door set into rich red brick, and ivy-covered walls. As soon as I rang the bell the door was opened. Holly beamed a welcoming smile, and Jim appeared just behind her. "Come in! How wonderful that you're here."

Holly and I reached out to hug each other immediately. I was struck with both the joy of meeting her and a powerful sense of recognition. I "knew" her and that was all there was to it. I felt as if I had reconnected with a long-sought part of myself.

"This is Jim," Holly said, almost shyly, adding, "he's much younger than I am. I just wanted to explain that early on!"

Jim grinned and thrust forward a friendly hand, "Welcome. We're so glad you're here."

He suggested dinner, and a few minutes later we were settled in a comfortable booth in the an attractive neighborhood cafe. The tantalizing aroma of Chinese cookery teased our noses. The atmosphere was soothing, and my sense of urgency began to drift away. Our chatter became less rushed.

"I must tell you about this wonderful husband of mine," Holly stated. "We first met in California, eight years ago." As their story unfolded, Carol Ann and I became caught up by the ever-delightful romance and intrigue of two people finding each other. Both talking, each dipped into and embellished the other's memories. Working in the space industry—Jim was a scientist, Holly a secretary—they met, fell in love, and married in California. Several years later Jim was offered a teaching position at Purdue University, and they moved to Lafayette.

Jim was a quiet man, unassuming. I was struck by his kindness and his obvious love and appreciation for Holly. They had each experienced a failed previous marriage. Holly had two children: a son, James, and a daughter, Christina, and was a grandmother.

"Actually, I've lived three different lives," Holly said. She spoke of her early years spent in New York with her mother, Elise Ford, and "Poppy" as a blissful time. She was secure in their love, doted on, rejoiced in. "We had an apartment a few blocks from the Hotel des Artistes. Poppy came to see us every day, or we went to his studio, where my mother posed for him. She was so beautiful and sweet, never losing her temper. I thought she was an angel. I made a drawing of her as an angel when I was barely in school. I still have it." Holly paused, old feelings surfacing along with the memories. "They were so happy. They were always together, happy and laughing. There was so much joy."

As she spoke, I pictured the three of them. Christy, who was an established and sought-after artist of sixty-plus years, Elise in her early twenties and a stunning Ziegfield beauty, and their daughter, Holly Christina—the focus of their combined worlds. Christy had married Nancy Palmer in 1919 and remained married to her until his death in 1952. I hesitated to question Holly too closely on the relationships in the Christy scenario.

As if she could read my thoughts, Holly continued."I saw Nancy only a few times. She always disappeared, at least when we were in his studio." She looked away for a moment, and then added, "I remember something that happened back then. I was curious about her. I sneaked off upstairs one day when the maid told me no one was home. I peeked into her bedroom. There were dolls everywhere, dolls all over her bed and the chairs and the floor. It gave me the strangest feeling. I scooted out in a hurry." Holly smiled, a bit ruefully, after a moment. "It was a long time ago."

Her voice was edged with sadness as she continued, "I once went back to New York after Poppy died. I wanted to talk with Nancy, and I tried to see her. But she wouldn't answer my knock on the door. She knew I was there. The doorman had called her. She refused to speak to me."

Holly shook her head and continued with a smile, "There's so much I want to show you when we get back home. I have a videotape showing scenes from Poppy's summer place in Vermont.

Those were the best times of all."

"How did you find out Christy was your father?" Carol Ann asked, voicing the question I had longed to put into words.

"I was thirty-five years old when I discovered that the information on my birth certificate was wrong," Holly answered, and paused. "I had always been called Holly Morris, but my father's name on the birth certificate read Benjamin Ford. My mother and Poppy said my father was a war correspondent, and I presumed he'd been killed in combat."

Her eyes grew large, and took on a soft, luminous quality. "All I ever wanted was for Poppy to be my father," she continued, "and one day, I finally asked him about it. I remember exactly what I said: 'Why can't I call you Father?'" Holly took a sip of tea, far away now, at a distant time and place. "His answer was, 'You can call me Poppy, just like your mother does,'" Holly's voice was even, but I thought I caught a slight tremor in her hand as she again lifted her cup.

"Tell them about Uncle Jim," Jim gently prompted her.

She nodded. "After I grew up I wanted more than ever to know my real identity. I went to New York to see Aunt Doris, my mother's sister. They were always very close, and Doris, too, modelled for Poppy. In fact, I think Poppy painted her into the Café des Artistes murals.

"Doris was beautiful, in a way even more so than my mother. I was hoping that Doris would tell me about my birth. She and my grandmother were with my mother, on the Virginia coast, when I was born."

The noise in the restaurant had quieted. I glanced around quickly, not wanting to break the spell of Holly's words by even a movement. Most of the diners had gone. Across the room an Oriental family sat laughing together, spinning Chinese noodles expertly around chopsticks.

"Doris lived in a large double duplex on Central Park. I had only a day or so to be there. I got right to the point. I begged her to tell me the truth about my father." Holly's words stopped abruptly. She took a deep breath as if to summon strength and went on. "I pleaded with her. 'What would it matter *now*?' I kept asking. She said, 'Perhaps we'll discuss it later.' She wouldn't budge an inch.

I felt miserable. I finally gave up. I was furious and frustrated and hurt. Just as I was leaving, Uncle Jim came in. He knew I was in town and had driven over to see me. He's a brother of my mother and Doris."

"I asked him if we could talk together, alone. He could see how upset I was and he walked outside with me. I was crying and he put his arm around me. I just blurted out, 'Please, Uncle Jim, was Poppy my father?' He told me right then and there. 'Of course, he was.' I will never forget his kindness," Holly paused again, shook her head as if to clear it, and said, "I haven't thought about all this in a long time. But in some subtle way it's always with me."

We returned to the Longuski home, where Holly had unearthed scrapbooks, family pictures, and Christy prints. They were spread out on the dining room table.

There were original art works displayed throughout the downstairs area but no Christy paintings. "I'm an artist, too," Holly said, "I did this one." She pointed to a charming female nude study. "My mother was a fine painter in her own right," she continued. "She had a show in the Grand Central Galleries in New York City. She was trained as an interior designer, too, at Parsons School of Design. But of course Poppy was her real instructor. She won a most promising young artist award one year and did landscapes and portraits in a style much like his."

Throughout the house, patterns and prints in upholstery fabrics, rugs, and lampshades were combined into an eye-pleasing whole. I could see Holly's artistry at work. The stairway caught my attention. Warm, brown paisley wallpaper led upstairs. I walked over for a closer look. Framed snapshots marched up the landing. Here was Poppy. Here was Elise. Holly wandered over, noticing my interest. "I don't have a single painting of Poppy's," she told me in a voice rimmed with regret, "but I do have a lot of other keepsakes, for instance, these pictures."

I studied the faces before us. A wave of energy flowed through me. I felt electrified, the atmosphere seemed charged, although nothing unusual was happening. A strong sense of "something important is here" settled in. I didn't question the sensation. If I had whiskers, I smiled to myself, they'd be twitching. I looked at a profile of Christy sketched by his famous friend, James Montgomery Flagg. It was a wonderful companion piece to Flagg's rendering of Christy which hung by the bar at the Café des Artistes.

"There's a wonderful story about how my parents met," Holly broke in. "Poppy loved to dress up for parties and big society bashes. He went to a fancy costume ball one evening. My mother was there, dressed as Robin Hood. He took one look at her, and fell for her right then!"

Holly's voice was radiant, warm with her memories. "He always said, 'Holly, be happy. Love life. Enjoy being a woman, a female. Delight in your femininity. Be free. Run as fast as you can in the wind. Climb the mountain to its very top. Experience all that life offers, all of it. Know joy.'" Her exuberance was contagious. I laughed and agreed with her.

My eyes travelled a few steps upward. "What about this picture?" I asked, peering at it more closely. It seemed out of place, somehow, amid the Christy collection. It was a photograph of an artist painting a portrait of a distinguished beribboned and decorated officer. I recognized neither the man, nor the setting. "Is there another artist in the family?" I asked Holly, "and where's that beautiful room?"

Holly glanced nonchalantly at the photo. "Oh, that's Aunt Doris' duplex. Remember, I told you about it. In fact, Leona Helmsley will live there when she's released from prison. She bought the apartment from Doris some years ago and turned it into the Park Lane Hotel. This is what it looked like when Doris and her husband lived there."

The intriguing sense of anticipation prickled into life again. "Is this artist Doris' husband?" I asked.

Holly had already walked back down the few stairs and into the dining room. She called over her shoulder, "Yes. That's Tod. He was a very fine painter himself. Tod Styka." The name triggered a reaction somewhere in my mind, as if a long-forgotten door had clicked open. I shook my head, trying to grasp whatever it was that floated just outside my memory.

"Who did you say?" I asked Holly.

"Her husband's name was Styka. He was Polish," she answered back, sorting through a pile of memorabilia.

Carol Ann and Jim had joined her in the dining area. They were both absorbed in the stack of pictures and prints which Holly had spread before them. My eyes registered the scene at the table below, but my mind was busily toying with the elusive name, Styka. Then clarity burst through. Scene after scene unfolded as though on a mental movie screen. I saw the portrait of *The Christ,* the *Peace on Earth* and *Resurrection* paintings at the Biblical Arts Center in Dallas, then the giant canvas, *The Crucifixion* at Forest Lawn, and finally, unmistakably, I heard again the name, "Gamaliel." For an instant, I glimpsed the whole picture. I "knew," not with a mind or brain, but through a heartfelt, inner experience what had brought me to this place. As quickly as it had come, the canvas dissolved. The pieces fell, the links in a chain separated into individual parts. I struggled for composure.

"Come on down," I heard Holly repeat her invitation. "Come and look at these things." I couldn't speak. I studied again the picture of Styka. Was he the artist of *The Crucifixion*?

"Helen?" Holly was looking up at me curiously."What are you doing?"

"Holly, do you know anything about a famous painting in California called *The Crucifixion*?"

She paused a few moments, thinking it over, and then a smile of recognition appeared across her face. "Oh, yes, I know what you're talking about. Tod was the son of Jan Styka who painted that huge religious canvas. It's somewhere around L.A."

"It's at Forest Lawn," I answered, stunned again by the synchronicity. I realized that I had not told Holly much about my own quest. I had been far too engulfed in her history and experiences.

"Why did you ask about Styka?" Holly asked, "Have you heard of him? Have you seen his painting?"

"Yes," I began slowly, "the Biblical Arts Center in Dallas—it might not be there except for Styka's painting. Christy's religious paintings are there. And *The Christ* portrait. It's *my* story, finding them. I learned about Styka then." My voice trailed off.

"Wait, I don't understand," Holly implored.

"This is an incredible coincidence," I continued. I looked back to the wall of photographs. "Do you mean that one sister, Elise, was with Christy, and the other was Styka's wife?"

Holly joined me on the landing, looking at me closely. "That's right. Both sisters. Both artists."

"And they have been brought together, here on your wall."

"Well, yes, that's true," she answered, still quizzical.

I turned to face her. "Now I know why I've come, why we've been brought together, Holly.

As we sat in their living room, I attempted to describe several of what I called my "Christy miracles." I remembered the copy of Wapnick's book in the car. I brought it in to show Holly. She seemed to shrink back a bit when I handed it to her.

"I'm somewhat skeptical about religion," she said, eyeing the paperback. I had told her only a little about my search for Christy's portrait of Christ. I had sketched in a few aspects of my fascination with the painting when we had first talked by phone on Saturday morning. "Did you think I was some sort of religious fanatic?" I asked her.

"Well, to tell you the truth, I did wonder." Holly was obviously trying to be tactful.

"I was afraid of that," I confessed. "But I gave up trying to explain it a long time ago. It may not make sense in worldly terms, but miracles surely do happen. Seeing the picture of Styka on your wall is a perfect example, and connecting with you is another one. I can't turn away from the miracle of being in this room with you and Jim tonight either. Anyway, this is the painting of Christ which started the whole thing."

Holly picked up the Wapnick book, as though weighing it. "I mentioned that I'd had three lives earlier," she said reflectively, "the first was with my mother and Poppy, the last one, of course, has been my years with Jim, and the second—

"I married a man I met when I lived in Washington, D.C. He was handsome and charming, and I was very young and insecure. He was from a Mexico City family. After we married, we moved there."

Holly got up and began to walk about the room. She stood before the fireplace, continuing, "After a few years I was miserable. My husband became attracted to a religious group and it gradually took over our lives. The leader of the group—actually I thought it was more of a cult— took my husband under his wing. At first, it was exciting. People were contributing huge sums of money for religious crusades. This evangelist had his own private jet. We flew with him all over the country and to Europe. We entertained and were entertained royally." Holly paused and sat down beside Jim.

"We were jet-setting with rich and famous people and all that goes with that kind of lifestyle," she continued a wry smile, "and then I began to have doubts. I got suspicious about where all the money was going." Holly picked up the book and looked intently at the painting of Christ. "This man was billed as a savior, a great leader who would serve mankind, and so forth. But he was a hypocrite. He preached about morals and family values and good deeds, but in reality he was funneling a lot of the money sent in by admirers into his own pocket. And not only that," Holly's eyes flashed with anger, "this model of virtue was abusing his own daughter. She told me what was happening. It made me sick.

"I was angry, furious at the hypocrisy and subterfuge, the duping of the people. I couldn't believe in that kind of religion. So I left. I took my children and got out with nothing, no money, nothing. But I didn't care. I went to California and found a job. I started a new life," she hesitated and sighed. "The whole experience left me with resentment of religion and Christianity and churches and theology and God. And that really began my search for 'myself,' my own identity." She sighed again. "I searched for a long time, tried many things. Read a lot, studied. I did all the things one does to find help, to get clarity. And then one day, I met Jim. We started together in building over our lives."

Jim smiled in agreement, "I'd had some rough years, as well. In fact, strangely enough, I had also been married to a Mexican. An interesting coincidence."

Holly looked from Jim to Carol Ann and me, "I'm still somewhat skeptical when I hear about someone's religious experiences—or see something like this book." She paused. "And what does this mean? This *Course in Miracles* printed on the cover? Is it some new spiritual path?"

I shifted uneasily, trying to frame a simple answer. "Well, yes, I suppose it is. But, Holly, I understand your feelings very well.

I've gone through so much of what you've described in my own life, in my own way. I've had so many doubts. I still do. This "Christy Quest," as I call it, is a major part of my search for answers."

And what of Christy's own quest? Why did he turn from sensual art to religious art? I had heard that Christy was struck by blindness in the early 1940s. Terrified and confused, the artist prayed for help. If his sight was restored, he vowed to paint the visions that were then appearing to him. Miraculously, he began to see again. The five spiritual works of the last decade of his life came forth: *The Christ, The Nativity, Peace on Earth, The Resurrection, Christ After Chaos: The Prince of Peace,* and *The Christ Commission.*

Holly confirmed the story. Then after a pause, she said, "We can talk more in the morning. Let's watch the video now." Carol Ann and I both readily agreed. It had been an intense evening and a break felt right. Jim crossed to the TV, inserted the Christy tape, dimmed a lamp, and we sat back to watch.

The TV screen flared into life. Here was another miracle: an opportunity to watch the figure who had intrigued me for so long. I felt like I did when I glimpsed an eclipse or stood at the top of a high ski lift. I was half afraid to look, as much as I wanted to.

The film was running—black and white home movies spliced together. Scene after scene of Holly's babyhood appeared. She was adorable, plump and laughing as she cavorted in a swimming pond, dressed in sunsuit and bonnet. Elise, a beautiful and tender mother, held her protectively. I remember the Nativity painting and Elise, the perfect choice as Mary. When I had mentioned the canvas earlier, Holly indicated that her mother not only posed as Christy's Mary, but as the background figure of Joseph as well. Elise's beauty was remarkable. On film she seemed even lovelier than her photographs.

I watched as she played with her baby and several shots later, as she posed for Christy. I thanked whoever had reached for the movie camera at that moment, catching the two together as they worked. Christy, robed in an artist's smock, sat before an unfinished canvas. His left hand darted easily from palette to painting, chatting as he brush-stroked details into his work. Elise posed prettily, her slender hands laced together, elbows on a draped table. Suddenly, he motioned to her, "Come and see." She swirled up and around quickly, almost like a colt in youthful enthusiasm, pleasure written in her eyes.

Their affection for each other was communicated unmistakably. How could anyone doubt they were in love? The reel wound on: scenes of rural beauty, frame after frame of Christy teaching Holly to swim, of friends and neighbors frolicking and splashing in the Vermont mill pond, of Christy proudly displaying his latest landscapes.

"These pictures were taken in Vermont, in Pawlet," Holly broke in. "Here's the dam that Poppy built himself." Christy, in swimming trunks, held a wiggling Holly in his arms.

"He adored you," I said. "Look how you delighted him."

"He wrote some wonderful poetry to me," she answered.

An excerpt from Movietone News appeared: "President's Mother Thanks Artist for Birthday Poster" Here was an aged Sara Roosevelt smiling with the artist as they stood before a real-life depiction of the poster mentioned. Elise, as the "Spirit of Victory," stood with her arms about a boy and girl, the visage of FDR himself looking up toward them. How could a person or a population not be moved by a beautiful woman representing the American spirit, whether carrying a blazing torch or shepherding children? Elise became a symbol of national pride in those years. She revealed a purity and strength of character the nation needed. And Christy was a chronicler-on-canvas of American history. His huge painting, *The Signing of the Constitution,* had brought acclaim and was exhibited in the U.S. Capitol. The trumpet call-to-arms continually sounded through his posters.

"Poppy did four poster-paintings for President Roosevelt," Holly stated. "I think my mother was in all of them."

A home movie scene came next. Holly was growing up into a shyly smiling pig-tailed charmer of perhaps seven or eight years. Next to her stood Poppy, beaming with fatherly pride. His showmanship was obvious. He always loved a spotlight and was a born performer. His canvases exhibited the same exuberance and flair for drama.

Christy was known as a womanizer who pursued many of his models. His flagrant lifestyle became a part of his persona. Newspapers and magazines carried tales of his indiscretions. The artist seemed to relish the notoriety and did not contradict it. I wondered if the blazing rancor of his first divorce made him reluctant to leave Nancy, his second wife. However she felt and whatever she knew of his liaisons, Nancy chose to look away from them. She remained Christy's staunch supporter, his companion and champion until his death in 1952.

What this must have cost her privately, one could only surmise. She herself had come into Christy's life at age sixteen, a hopeful young model-to-be who had been turned down by Charles Dana Gibson. Gibson had considered her too "overblown" for his illustrations and sent her, instead, to Christy who accepted her immediately, sketching her into hundreds of illustrations, paintings, portraits, and posters. Hers was the face which enticed the youth of America into military service during the years of World War I.

Christy soon brought her from New York to his Ohio Barracks and married her not long after his divorce from Maybelle. Nancy adored her partnership in Christy's fame. She loved the excitement of meeting celebrities, the splendid trips, and the lavish studio apartment in the Hotel des Artistes. It must have been painful, indeed, when her place was usurped by a much younger, more beautiful, and artistically talented model named Elise Ford.

Nancy, who had years earlier replaced Maybelle Thompson Christy in the artist's affections, now knew herself the humiliation of being cast aside. For Elise, as these movies indicated, was not just another model to be seduced. She was special. She became an inherent part of Christy's life from their first encounter, even bearing him a child. But Nancy stayed.

"A Visit to Mt. Vernon—Howard, Elise, and Doris" read the screen. "She really *is* gorgeous," I gasped, at the first glimpse of "Aunt Doris." The Ford sisters stood side by side, laughing and chatting with Christy, as the camera recorded them. Elise and Doris were obviously sisters, closely alike in bone structure and coloring, but Doris stood a bit taller and her beauty spoke more of sophistication and polish than did the youthful scrubbed-clean image of Elise.

Now Christy appeared with a highly decorated naval officer,

Christy and Elise

the famous grin in place. With a battleship in the background, scenes of a happy group enjoying an afternoon yachting excursion came next. Elise looked adorable, a perky version of a sailor's cap perched on her head.

"I feel as though I'm getting to know Christy and Elise, watching them together," I said to Holly.

The tape offered further scenes from Holly's childhood, some in color—a beach in Virginia, a skating rink in Central Park, and more views of the Vermont vacation home. Finally, a last glimpse of Holly appeared as a toddler, splashing among riverbed rocks in childlike absorption, oblivious to the camera.

"Happy times," Holly reminisced, as the film played out. Jim stood to retrieve the tape, flicked on a lamp, and I sat quietly savoring what we had seen. My heart was full, too, with a gratitude I couldn't begin to express. Then a weariness struck me as we all stood up and stretched. It was time to go. We said a final goodnight to Holly and Jim, and walked down the sidewalk to-

Holly

ward the car. I turned to wave back once more as we drove away. Holly and Jim stood together, framed in the doorway's glow.

"Come over now and we'll go out for breakfast," Holly said when I called her early the next morning. "There's someone I want you to meet."

Curiosity spurred me into action, and we sped off soon after. Once settled in a coffee shop, we scanned the menu.

"Who are we going to meet?" asked Carol Ann.

"Her name is Mary Bone," said Holly. "She's an aunt on Poppy's mother's side of the family. She lives on a few acres outside of town."

This was an unexpected bonus. Not only Christy's daughter, but an aunt as well.

"How did you meet her?" I asked Holly.

"It was another interesting coincidence," she explained. "An artist friend here was asking me about my background in art. I mentioned Poppy. He said he knew of a woman who had a family connection to him. I called her, and she invited me out right away." Holly paused for a bite of toast and went on. "She's elderly, a retired school teacher, a grand person, bright and sharp and fun to be with. You'll like her."

"Does she remember Poppy?" I asked.

Not really," Holly returned, "but she does know a lot about the Bone family, and she has a genealogy chart."

I had wondered what the Christy-Bone relatives would think of Holly. Aunt Mary, at least, had seemed to welcome her into the family.

The conversation shifted and Holly's eyes clouded. "I was with Poppy the night before he died. He called and asked me to come for dinner in the Café, just the two of us. It was a wonderful several hours. He told me that I was the most important person in his life and never to forget it, that I'd always been his greatest joy. This is the first time I've been able to talk about that evening without crying. His legs were so swollen with edema. He was quite ill, but still cheerful and optimistic. He died the next morning.

"Poppy drank, you know." Holly brought up another painful subject.

"Yes, I first heard about that from Norris Schneider," I answered. "He was, from the sound of it, an alcoholic."

"Yes," Holly agreed, "but I never saw him touch a drink. Never. And my mother didn't drink either."

I told Holly about my conversation with Mimi Miley, a curator at the Allentown, Pennsylvania, art museum. In 1976 Mimi created the first large-scale Christy exhibit since the artist's death. I discovered "the Mimi connection" through Schneider's notes.

Mimi's mother, Jane Conneen, was a sister-in-law to Nancy Christy's second husband, Bob Conneen. I telephoned Mimi early in my Christy search. She, too, had indicated reports of Christy's drinking. Although the Conneen family did not have contact with Christy, they were close to Nancy after she married Bob. "She was like a grandmother to me," Mimi said. After Bob's death, the Conneens gathered whatever remained in the Hotel des Artistes studio and brought it to Pennsylvania.

"I wonder—" Holly put in. "Should I try to contact Mimi? I'd love to see some of Poppy's things."

I nodded an eager "yes" to her question, and searched my overstuffed shoulder bag for the Christy address list I always carried. The waitress reappeared, "More coffee?" Carol Ann glanced at her watch, and I knew from her look that we should be on our way.

"Let's go," I agreed.

We quickly paid our bill and walked out into the blue-skied Indiana morning. The weather, warm and sunny, enhanced the countryside. We were soon on an Indiana farm road, and then turning into Aunt Mary's wide yard. Her house was a picture of Norman Rockwell's America, painted white with a big front porch. We parked under huge old trees. A black iron kettle held bright pansies, and a cat as black as the kettle strolled out to welcome us.

Holly rang the bell and after a moment, an attractive elderly lady opened the door. Aunt Mary was, true to Holly's description, exceedingly sharp. She walked us through her home proudly.

"These are the Christy prints, in here," Mary stated, leading us into a turn-of-the-century parlor. It was a perfect setting for the framed prints, and she spoke of each one fondly.

As an illustrator, Christy had been incredibly prolific, often sketching out a finished piece in one day. I had been collecting the books he'd illustrated for some months when David gave me a complete set of James Whitcomb Riley's wonderful volumes. Riley's poems were simple, heartfelt, warm, and homespun. They were dearly loved by the American reading public, as were the accompanying Christy illustrations. My favorite of these was titled *Out To Old Aunt Mary's.*

A sense of serenity wreathed the atmosphere, a feeling of perfection that had a "meant to be" quality. I thought about Gamaliel's advice: "Wait and see. If it's supposed to happen, it will happen. Nothing can stop the Truth."

A Soldier's Dream was the first of these drawings, and the one which produced his earliest acclaim. In it, a Christy girl entices her soldier-sweetheart in his dreams. On Mary's wall, I saw another picture—an elderly couple held their dream tightly: mentally and emotionally they were two starry-eyed young lovers.

"Christy was a true romantic," I heard myself say. "I guess that's one of the main reasons I'm so drawn to him."

I sat back quietly during the trip into town, content to watch fields and furrows skim by. An occasional distant tractor plowed its orderly path. Carol Ann and Holly chatted, but I heard little of their conversation. Holly had introduced several intriguing new characters into the Christy script: the Stykas, Jan and Tod; Doris and her daughter, Wanda; Uncle Jim, who still lived in New York state; and Aunt Mary Bone.

Questions about each one churned, surfacing for attention. The old obsession to "know" whispered its enticement. "Relax," I instructed myself. "There is time. The answers will come. Stop pushing."

I thought again about the perfection of the process, the unmistakable synchronicity which had appeared along with Holly. Had we met in Columbus, it would have been dramatic and informative, but I now knew how important this trip to Lafayette was. I needed to be in Holly's home, to see first-hand the Christy artifacts, the video and certainly the wall of photographs which had re-introduced Styka so powerfully. Holly and I needed to miss each other earlier, precisely so that we could connect later in this manner.

Gratitude poured its warmth into the moment. "The magic is in the unfolding," I heard the words clearly—where they came from didn't seem to matter. But I had an idea that my friend, Gamaliel, had returned.

"Okay," said Holly back at her house, "let's get to work." We were seated around the oval dining table. Its entire surface was covered with Christy memories, a lifetime stacked and spread before us. "You know what I'll do?" Holly offered, indicating the mass of material with a wide sweep of her hands. "I'll copy whatever you want me to and send it to you. Then you can study it at your leisure."

"That would be great," I nodded, turning through the 300-plus pages of Elise's diary.

"Hey!" Carol Ann suddenly called out. "Here's Babe Ruth, and John Philip Sousa, and Mrs. Sousa, and Fritz Kreisler and Eddie Rickenbacker and Will Rogers!"

Holly laughed. "Yes, I know. Poppy surprised my mother with that book for Christmas. He went around gathering notes and autographs, and then put them into that book for her to keep. She was thrilled."

I marveled again at the panorama of characters; so many were history-makers. The richness of the tapestry was intriguing. I thought of the Café des Artistes, the meeting place from which a creative chemistry poured forth in conversations and ideas. Christy had been the Hotel's first resident.

From its beginning until the present, the Café magnetized those whose artistic dreams had brought fame in one creative field or another. Politicians and sports figures frequented #1 West 67th Street, their combined talents adding to the synergistic brew.

Was there anyplace like it? I wondered. The Algonquin's historic Round Table drew the literary crowd, but they flocked to the Café, as well: Robert Benchley, Dorothy Parker, Heywood Broun, and Alexander Woolcott were only a few of these frequent visitors. The Chelsea group came also, and many from Paris.

As the afternoon wore on, we continued sifting through first one pile of articles, then another stack of pictures and prints, and another, and another. I forgot everything, lost again in the joy of discovery. The immediacy of the present was laced by the documents of the past. There was no separation of time or space. Christy might as well have joined us bodily, adding a bit of overlooked data here, a grin of assent—"Yes, that's correct"—or a wagging finger, "You're off track on that one."

Finally it was time to leave. Plans were made to meet again. My commitment to this Christy Quest, wherever and whatever it might lead to, was stronger than ever.

I left Holly's home with a trace of I-wish-I-could-stay-longer, but the overriding feeling was one of gratitude. There would be other trips and other meetings. This initial connection had been powerful, ripe in perfect timing, and rich with the possibilities of "tomorrow."

On our way home from Ohio and Indiana, Carol Ann and I explored Kentucky's lush horse farms and verdant rolling hills. We visited the "My Old Kentucky Home" State Park, which is situated several miles outside the small town of Bardstown. A gentle rain greeted us. Umbrellas unfurled, we entered the visitor's center. It was crowded and noisy with fellow tourists. We bumped and browsed for a few minutes in the gift shop and left.

A gravel walkway led through spacious grounds and ended at the top of a gentle hill crowned by a red-brick Southern mansion. Inside, a cadre of hoop-skirted ladies and men in antebellum garb greeted us. We asked about Christy's painting and were told of its location upstairs, "on the landing." Only a few sightseers wandered the halls. We climbed carpeted stairs framed by the luster of an old polished wood balustrade and arrived in a broad area, a point from which other rooms radiated.

The *I Dream of Jeannie* painting hung above a spinet piano. Christy's portrayal of composer Stephen Foster was indeed a beautiful work. Filled with drama and emotion, it was a painting of the heart. Young Foster sits at his piano, facing outward in contemplation of old southern scenes and the music flowing through his mind. An angel or muse of music floats above him, her forehead lighted by a star and her graceful arms reaching to touch him.

Christy had conceived a number of such portraits. He had surrounded Thomas Alva Edison with symbols of light and sound; ace Eddie Rickenbacker with the planes of World War I; Franklin Roosevelt sat ringed by the upturned faces of children. Steamboats, black field hands, Southern belles, cotton, and moonlit magnolias filled this vision of "Jeannie." The unmistakable visage of Elise appeared as Foster's "Spirit of Music." The setting was perfect.

I thought of the similarities joining Foster and Christy. Both had been determined from youth to pursue their careers, and in the face of powerful odds. The Christys of small-town Ohio, though rich in familial affection, were poor financially. Stephen Foster's upbringing took place in a socially-prominent home, yet he was constantly berated and discouraged by his parents in following his musical dreams. Both plowed on through numerous hardships and setbacks.

A "Christy"had appeared in Foster's life. Colonel E. P. Christy, who created the famous "Christy Minstrel" shows, believed in the talent of young Foster. His black-faced choruses sang and played Foster's music. Both Christy and Foster were alcoholics. Foster died at age thirty-eight, penniless and shamed into oblivion by the disease. Christy lived almost eighty years, plunging from time to time into the depths of alcoholic depression.

It was closing time at the mansion. Carol Ann put away her camera, as I did my Christy memories. We left Stephen Foster to continue dreaming of "Jeannie" and walked outside into the misty Kentucky afternoon.

The Christy Quest continued to gain steam after the Ohio trip. Doors opened. Opportunities appeared to explore. I rented a post office box and placed ads in several newspapers asking for information about Christy. The response was gratifying. Information came from New York, California, Florida—and even nearby Fort Worth. Several Bone relatives wrote from Ohio. A Christy collector I had longed to contact sent a warm response from California.

David gave me printed business cards with *Illustrations des Artistes* scripted above my name and address. I was thrilled and had stationery printed so I could reply in style to the incoming mail. I also registered the *Artistes* name as my trademark. I now had a real "Christy business."

Some time earlier I had begun to visit antique shops, malls, and hideaways in search of Christy books, prints, and posters. From my first purchase of twelve small Christy illustrations in Granbury, Texas, a flood of "finds" came forth. I was soon out of space in closets and drawers. I found a map chest perfect for storing larger prints and posters. A bedroom became the "Christy

Room." As correspondence increased, I employed a part-time secretary, Melinda Segal, who kept me organized and up to date with new purchases.

Notebooks burgeoned. My photcopying costs soared. I cut back on expenditures in other areas, happy to do so. I felt like a twenty-one-year old graduate with a brand-new degree in hand, eager to explore a chosen field. The truth was, of course, I was fifty-five years old, my degree long lost in a dusty attic. Yet I had never known such joy. My self-esteem, bruised and flagging in earlier years, became stronger. Gradually, and sometimes still timidly, I made telephone calls, took trips, and wrote letters of inquiry to possible Christy sources. I clung to the powerfully succinct Nike® slogan, "Just do it!" The side effect of the whole process was simply pleasure. I was having fun, more fun than I could have imagined. Whatever all of it was leading to, or what it was "about," dimmed in the light of the current Christy miracle. I felt my life had been transformed into *A Course in Miracles*.

This was not theoretical nor abstract; it was real. I was becoming content with the journey and its unfoldment, no longer frantically scrambling about for an end result or "product." With acceptance came new forms of creativity. Possibilities peeked around corners.

I was blessed by encouragement and support everywhere I turned. Each new Christy cohort expressed enthusiasm and curiosity. It was contagious, this adventure. I loved meeting fellow art patrons, antique dealers, the many people who had Christy memories and/or artifacts, either in person or on paper. There was energy here, inherent in the network of shared interest.

Holly and I talked often over the year, frequently several times a week. Her life, too, was opening in unexpected ways. Her feeling of self-worth escalated along with my own. Our friendship flourished. Our mutual dream was a trip to New York City together. The Café des Artistes offered its magnetic pull. But first I had a serendipitous interlude.

In September 1992, David and I flew to Hawaii. We planned to spend two weeks on five islands. Our high-rise hotel in Honolulu was perched on the edge of Ala Moana Beach. Big windows provided a sweeping view of the ocean. Farther down to the left, Diamondhead's craggy profile jutted up from the water. As with every trip I took, I wondered what and if any Christy clues would appear. I knew that Christy had not visited these islands. There seemed to be no obvious connections here. But I had been surprised before.

Hurricane Iniki struck the islands the day after we arrived. I had never experienced the power of wind and surf combining into the huge breakers which whipped our beach. Palm trees bowed and broke. Litter filled the air. We were corralled into the hotel's ground floor for several hours.

Later, David and I explored the islands in tiny rental cars. Each one bravely bounced us over the back roads and mountain passes. The views were stunning, just as the guidebooks described. Flowers and waterfalls and pineapple fields appeared around every curve of the road.

One of our last stopovers was Hilo. David had told me of the interesting and beautiful flowers, plants, and trees which abounded throughout these tropical lands. I was eager to see banyan trees. These were nature's pranks encased in wood. Each tree sprouted massive trunk and bough formations which defied reason. They were extraordinary.

We turned into the drive leading to our hotel, the Hilo Hawaiian, late one afternoon, tired and dusty from another long day of exploring. "You'll love this place," David announced, pointing to the sign beside the entrance which read "Avenue of Trees." Each tree was a stalwart banyan. Both sides of the long drive were lined with these sentinels. They presented a magnificent prelude to the bay which appeared at the end of their leafy tunnel. David drove slowly down the avenue, allowing me to look at each tree.

"Not just one or even several banyans, but a whole forest of them!" I marveled. I noticed that each tree had a placard affixed to its trunk printed with a different name and date. It seemed to be a special tribute of some kind. The names were of world-known figures, from Eleanor Roosevelt to Gandhi to Helen Keller. Suddenly, a name appeared which puzzled me momentarily: Fannie Hurst. The date below the name was July 17, 1935.

"David, stop the car!" I cried."Stop here!"

He glanced at me with alarm, pulling immediately to a halt on the roadside. "What is it? What's wrong?"

I was out of the car and crossing the road before I called back. "She must have planted this tree *on my birthday*!" I stood staring at the black print beneath the tree. The tingling sensation which was becoming more familiar— when something unexpected had happened, or was about to, that sense of "something important is here"—struck with surety.

As usual, I couldn't explain my increasing awareness in these moments. I just knew that I was meant to stand at Fannie Hurst's tree.

"Well, I'll be darned," David said at my shoulder. "It is your birthdate, exactly. And who is Fannie Hurst?"

I searched my memory vigorously. "I've heard her name, but I can't go further. I'll look it up as soon as I can."

During our two-day stay at the hotel, I continued to rack my mind as to her identity. Nothing came. "Fannie Hurst" remained intriguingly just out of reach. So far there had been no Christy connection on this Hawaiian trip. I wondered if this was it. Each time we passed Fannie's tree, I voiced a silent request, "What am I to learn from this?" My intuition rang with certainty. I relaxed, finally, and waited for Fannie Hurst to walk on stage.

I had been back home for several days, coping with jet-lag lethargy and the inevitable list of piled-up "things to do" before I began to tackle Christy research again. I was warm with memories of the Hawaiian sun, floral bounty, and delicious seafood.

Earlier in the year, I had discovered the writings of myth-collector Joseph Campbell. Campbell had lived on the Big Island and had grown to love it. His favorite spot was mentioned in his biography. It was a place to meditate in the shade of an immense banyan tree where he could watch the sun descend into the ocean. Campbell's search for truth had been summarized into a three-word statement: "Follow your bliss."

We had found Campbell's spot and walked into the beautiful lanai sheltered by the banyan tree. It was, as he had indicated, right on the beach. The ocean breakers rolled in softly, whispering a rhythmic cadence. Birds flew among the serpentine branches of the banyan. Serenity emanated from the air itself. A piece of heaven, I thought. Sitting there, shaded and protected by the massive arms of the tree, I resolved to continue my own journey toward both the meaning and the experiencing of "bliss"

I sighed a lingering "aloha" to the memory, and reached for the Café des Artistes cookbook which lay topmost on a stack of books beside my bed. After the first months of reading and re-reading the beautiful little volume, I had not spent much time with it. Now, I dipped into it with renewed interest.

A bookmark slid to the floor. I glanced at the page where it had been placed, pausing at a paragraph which spoke of the celebrated visitors to the Café. Among the listing of these, a name came into focus. The sentence read, "Fannie Hurst had her own table in the Café." I read the words again. Fannie, a popular novelist and short-story writer, had indeed taken her place in the Christy cast.

How many times have I searched these pages? I thought in wonderment, without picking up on her name? It didn't make sense. Yet, here she was, her presence announced in what I supposed was its own perfect timing.

I stretched to retrieve the heavy encyclopedia from its place by my bedside table: "Hurst, Fannie. . . ."

6

As so often happens on a flight to Manhattan, our plane circled LaGuardia Airport for more than an hour. I was frustrated. Reading magazines or working crossword puzzles didn't help. It was almost one o'clock and my appointment with Judy Goffman, a noted Christy expert, at the Gallery of American Illustrators was for three that afternoon.

"Will we ever get there?" I asked my traveling companion, Joan Duff. I hated the thought of being late for a first meeting with Judy. Finally, the pilot announced our descent. Gratefully, I began to breathe again.

Once on land, we headed toward the baggage claim area. The airport was packed with passengers and personnel. "How will we ever get a cab?" I wailed. The bags were heavy, the day hot, humid, and overcast. My mood matched the weather. Grumbling, I bent over in an effort to drag my bulkiest bag out of the stream of human traffic. Feeling a light tap on my shoulder, I straightened up and glanced around.

"Can I help you?" asked a large man, dressed in black suit and cap. "Do you need a taxi?" he continued. Did we!

"Let me take those," he amiably insisted, and I nodded thankfully.

A steady downpour greeted us outside. Our guardian-angel

driver sloshed purposefully ahead, laden with suitcases. In the parking garage, we arrived at a black limousine. Feeling like Cinderellas, we stepped into the cool leather interior of our carriage.

"We'll not only arrive in time, but in style!" I laughed to Joan. Allowing myself to relax at last, I thought ahead to the impending appointment.

I had initially seen Judy's name among Norris Schneider's Christy collection. She had written to him a decade earlier in the hope of receiving background information on the artist. As I delved more into research on Christy, I came across further references to Judy.

Her career had begun in a place which rang with the sound of a mythical kingdom: Blue Bell, Pennsylvania. She had taken a hobby—collecting illustrations, magazine covers, and prints—and turned it into a successful career. After moving to New York City, she purchased a historic brownstone on East 77th Street and created a charming and influential art gallery. Her collection of fine illustrators grew, as did her reputation. Most important in my mind, she was a Christy devotee.

It was still raining when our driver pulled up to the curb outside the Gallery of American Illustrators. With my notebook and camera, I climbed the several steps to the bright red front door while Joan went on to the hotel. An attractive young female face appeared at a huge side window with a smile and a motion to come inside. The door signal buzzed and I entered a marble foyer. A hall door opened, and the pretty face became Kristen Thomas, Judy's assistant.

"You must be Helen." She smiled graciously. "Judy is expecting you, of course, but she had to go to a funeral. She'll be here in thirty minutes or so."

My heart sank and I thought, she'll never get here. The afternoon traffic. The rain.

I'm sure Kristen read my poorly-disguised disappointment. She offered coffee and her own tour of the gallery. She pointed out the picture files. I meandered and browsed while she finished up some work.

The current exhibit focused on calendar art. These were the

pin-up queens of the 1940s. Their saucy smiles and scantily clad shapes adorned bedrooms, barrooms, and bombers. I was intrigued by the roster of famous artists' signatures. As a teenager, I had pored through magazines which displayed these curvaceous models in ads and short story illustrations—from Jon Whitcomb's starry-eyed heroines to those of Coby Whitmore and Alfred Parker. And here they were "in person," vivid and immediate. They were sexy in an outdoorsy way, likable and friendly—the girl-next-door as every girl then wanted to look. The loveliest of all posed coquettishly in her place on an easel. I wondered who she was.

I looked through Judy's Christy slides and the color photographs of paintings which she now owned or had sold. Here was Elise, exquisite in various settings, in pastoral scenes, on posters, and on a magnificent sectional screen. I was so enrapt I almost jumped when Kristen appeared at my side suggesting that we walk upstairs to the second-floor showroom.

I followed her up the marble steps and into a rather small room, simply furnished with an antique oak table and chairs. On every wall hung splendid oil paintings.

"These are Judy's living quarters," explained Kristen. "This is her dining area."

A huge Christy self-portrait hung on the widest wall. I had yearned to see this painting ever since spotting it in Susan Meyer's fine book, *Great American Illustrators.*

I stood for a moment hypnotized by the artist's face: a mane of graying hair, the strong jaw line, and the determined look in his eyes—the outer expression of what Christy saw within himself. His nude model sat in the background, her arms lifted, her face turned slightly toward the artist. His "sidekick" Elise looked as though she had been caught in a moment of contemplation.

Holly must see this, I thought, realizing that it was the only painting which portrayed Christy and Elise together. Painted in 1935, Christy was sixty-two years old, Elise in her twenties. I felt the chemistry, the electricity of their relationship as I studied the unfinished oil.

The artist was left-handed. His paint-decked palette, held in his right hand, was in the foreground. A red drape fell teasingly across Elise's bare legs. His eyes were riveting. I found it hard to turn away.

Kristen pointed out the room's companion pieces, a famous rendition of *Sleeping Beauty* by Maxfield Parrish, a Rockwell scene, a Leyendecker. She led me into an adjoining area, a vast, high-ceilinged and heavily-beamed room. A huge stone fireplace was built into a west wall and comfortable furnishings were arranged around it. There was a Tudor, or even medieval, feel to the room. The paneled walls were dark with old wood and hung with familiar paintings. A magnificent screen stood at the far end of the fireplace. It was a Christy tribute to Stephen Foster—a moonlit, star-bright scene, filled with music and lush female nudes.

In contrast to the massive sitting room, a small, brightly lit library opened off of the east wall. Filled with books and paintings, it held a sunny charm of its own.

Kristen glanced at her watch. "Judy should be here soon. Let's go downstairs and wait for her."

The large front window offered a view of still-falling rain. Kristen went back to her work. I glanced over the printed material she had pulled together describing the gallery and its history.

Suddenly, the door flew open. A tiny figure, damp, dewy, smiling, bustled into the room. "This is Judy," I thought, smiling in return. "What a wonderful face." Shimmering with energy, graceful and light on her feet, even raincoated and with a bulky bag in hand, she walked quickly across the room.

"Sorry about being late," she apologized.

"I'm so glad to see you at all," I answered.

Kristen handed Judy a few notes and telephone messages. She glanced at them, looked up, and said somewhat breathlessly, "Give me a few minutes and then we'll talk."

"Of course," I nodded. She hurried from the room, sparks flying behind her. I drank a few sips of fresh coffee, again perused the calendar girl exhibit, and waited.

Ten minutes later she was back, motioning an invitation to follow her upstairs. "Let's sit down by the fireplace," she suggested, as we once again entered the art-filled studio. She had just held successful exhibits in Rome and Japan, arranging for the first exhibit by an American illustrator in the Orient. The Japanese public had fallen in love with Norman Rockwell. Over 300,000 people had flocked to the galleries in three cities where his works had been shown. As she spoke about the exhibit, her eyes lit up with excitement. She hoped to include Christy paintings in a second exhibit to be held in Japan.

Bright, sharp-witted, intuitive and gifted, Judy was as attractive as she was blessed in intellect. Springy light-brown curls flowed down to her shoulders. A delicate path of freckles played across her cheeks, giving her face a gamine, saucy look.

We talked for some time about our joint interest. Judy's first artistic love had been Christy—he was the catalyst for her earliest collection and later for the gallery. She had begun to purchase work by Christy soon after his death. By that time his widow, Nancy, had married Bob Conneen, and Judy had befriended Bob after Nancy died.

Listening intently as she spoke of Christy's influence in her life, I felt I had found another cohort. I shared my own enthusiasm on finding *The Christ* and the joy which its discovery brought.

Christy's self portrait hung directly across from us in the dining alcove. I kept turning my head to look at it. His bearing and gaze were compelling. Surrounded by these Christy-filled walls, I said, "I feel as though he's here in the room with us."

Judy smiled in confirmation, "I certainly agree."

"I've felt guided since the beginning, since I first saw Christy's painting on the book cover," I continued. "Well, not only guided but pushed, propelled, thrust into the stream of Christy-consciousness."

"There is no doubt about that," Judy answered.

Turning to leave, I walked once again past the paintings in an effort to photograph them into my mind. Here was Elise as the "Spirit of Victory," scantily clad in sheer gauze, in one hand a cornucopia and the other a laurel wreath. "Stand by Your President" read the 1932 poster. Next to it hung the life-size portrait of a society grand dame. Dressed in black satin and holding an unfurled pink ostrich-feather fan, her provocative smile unmistakably stated her pleasure in posing.

An aging, yet elegant Christy girl, I thought. In contrast, the *American Dream House* presented a young couple, their baby held in the mother's arms and their wished-for cottage sketched high on the canvas, floating in their imagination. This was a demure Elise, but a no less intriguing one. Painted in 1937, I noticed. Two years before Holly's birth.

I studied Christy's self portrait. His eyes held a message. "Continue," they seemed to say. Voicing a silent assent, I said goodbye to Judy and floated out of the door. Sailing in winds of excitement, I wafted over to Madison Avenue and hailed a cab. It had stopped raining. A late afternoon sun speared through low-lying clouds. Whether rainbows actually appeared or not, I saw them.

During the cab ride to the hotel, my mind buzzed with images. Many were beautifully framed and strikingly arranged on softly lit walls, some were poised on easels, others were on slides. I was jubilant at seeing so many Christy works in one place at one time.

Judy had remarked that there were few people left who had known the artist. I had told her about Holly, who held vivid memories of "Poppy." Christy had painted portraits of Dr. and Mrs. Norman Vincent Peale. Dr. Peale, now in his nineties, was still writing and could be interviewed.

"There are others still alive who remember Christy. I know we'll find them," I had said.

That evening, as Joan and I were going to the Hotel des Artistes for dinner, I thought about Christy's studio there. He had decorated it after the style of his mentor and teacher, William Merritt Chase. An old-world opulence was created in #7 with beams, balconies, and bearskin rugs. The apartment was laden with paintings by Christy, tapestries, copper and bronze urns, heavy draperies, and innumerable objets d'art. The model of a sailing ship hung from a rafter. Nancy Palmer Christy kept every vase filled with fresh flowers.

The Hotel itself had been a milestone. It was one of the first buildings in New York City constructed to allow artists a home-plus-studio environment. Christy had been the first resident, moving there in 1917, even before it was finished. He remained in these studio quarters until his death in 1952. The Christys entertained often and sumptuously. I wondered if there had been a guest register. Nancy, unfortunately, did not keep a diary. I knew of no written memoirs of their years together; however, newspaper and magazine coverage offered a hint of the grandeur.

We walked into the Hotel and were at once surprised to see a disheveled old woman trudging into the lobby carrying a brown paper sack filled with whatever treasures she'd found on the streets. Her attitude reflected her attire: exhausted, torn, unclean and mismatched. And yet there was a sauciness, a pride about her as she dragged herself to an overstuffed chair and plumped down into it. However bedraggled and beaten, she looked as if she owned the place.

Joan and I stood at the Hotel entry staring in silence. Around us walked the well-dressed, sophisticated throng heading toward the Café. No one appeared to take any interest in, and certainly was not shocked by, the ragged old lady's presence.

We were seated at a small table in the Café directly across from the *Parrot Girl*. The unmistakable face and form of Elise gazed out from among palm fronds and other tropical plants. Several brilliantly plumed parrots perched on a branch. I had called for reservations three weeks earlier; I was determined to be in plenty of time *this* time. Also this time I hoped to meet the Langs. George Lang, world-famed restaurateur, had purchased the Café des Artistes in 1975. He had completely renovated the Café, and the menu reflected his expertise in fine food and wines.

In July, Libby Meyers, a close friend for years, gave me a birthday lunch. I casually remarked that I planned a trip to New York in October and was interested in the Christy murals at the Café des Artistes.

"The Café is one of our favorite restaurants," she responded. "We've been going there for years. In fact, I know someone who is a close friend to the Langs."

Surprised, I asked, "Who?"

"Her name is Susanna Fodor," Libby answered. "She's an attorney with Bob's law firm, the branch office in New York. She's Hungarian, beautiful and brilliant. She handled the Gundel's acquisition, a giant undertaking. You could ask her how to reach the Langs."

Gundel's was Lang's new restaurant in Budapest. After giving my request to talk with the Langs to Susanna, she had called me back to say that "George is in Budapest, at Gundel's. But Jennifer will stop by your table for a visit."

I sat thinking about my good fortune. It certainly fit with other such occurrences along the way. For one thing, it had come so naturally. I hadn't had to search either methodically or feverishly for an introduction to the Café owners. After my initial lesson in regard to the "lost" portrait of Christ, I had more or less relaxed into the "letting it happen" theory.

"What will be your choice for dinner?" asked the black-jacketed waitress expectantly. My mind returned to the moment: "Oh, give me a minute more," I said. She bowed and retreated, leaving us to scan the selections offered.

When our attentive waitress returned, I asked, "Is Mrs. Lang here?"

"No," she stated, "she came in earlier, and left awhile ago."

"Oh, no!" Disappointment stung my eyes.

"Helen," Joan answered, "this is the time you have to keep on believing—when something doesn't work out the way you want it to." Her words rang with truth, and the lump in my throat began to dissolve.

"You're right," I agreed, "and we have a wonderful evening before us."

Our waitress had reappeared. "I have an idea," she said, "Write a note to Mrs. Lang, and we'll try to get it to her."

I took out an *Illustrations des Artistes* card, jotted down a few sentences and handed it to her.

"It's the old lady in the lobby who interests me," Joan said. "I can't wait to ask someone about her."

Sometime later, while we were eating, I heard a voice. "Hello, I'm Jennifer Lang." I looked up in surprise.

"Tell me about your interest in the Café—and, I understand, in Christy."

"I—" where would I begin? How could I describe this "quest"? Gradually the words came.

"This is fascinating," Jennifer responded. "Perhaps I can be of help in some way."

I asked if there were any people still living who might have had contact with Christy. Jennifer took a few moments to think. "Yes," she stated. "I do know one person who knew him. Olga Steckler. I believe that she modeled for him. I'll give you her phone number. I'll give you Ruth Peabody's number also. She's the current president of the Hotel board."

We talked on some minutes longer. Jennifer's dark brunette hair was pulled back tightly from her face, caught into a fashionable chignon at her neck. She did not appear tall, but her straight carriage suggested confidence. "Call me at my office in the morning," she was saying, "I'll be there around ten. I'll give you the phone numbers then, and we'll talk more." I took the business card which she handed me. "I must get home to my son," she smiled and extended her hand for a friendly good-bye shake. A second later she was gone.

"Well, how about that?" prodded Joan, her eyes sparkling in amusement.

"You were right." I sighed. "I have to keep on believing."

"How about dessert?" the waitress asked, presenting us with menus. "This is the one for you," she grinned mischievously. "The Palette." I read further, finding its description, and succumbed immediately. Dedicated to Christy, it was made of tiny scoops of ice creams and sherbets spread upon a dish shaped like an artist's palette.

"Christy himself would approve," I said to Joan and glanced once again at the *Parrot Girl*, saucily posed across the room.

I took one last lingering look at the Christy murals on the Café walls as I walked from the restaurant into the Hotel lobby. Joan was already standing by the switchboard office, talking with the young man whom I guessed was the night manager. She had questioned him about the strange old lady whom we had seen earlier.

"Oh, that's Emma," he answered with a grin. "She lives here."

Joan and I exchanged surprised looks, both of us hoping for more information. The elevator doors opened and a uniformed operator stepped out to join us. "We were wondering about Emma," Joan offered, including him in the conversation.

"She's been here forever," he began. "She was the maid for a wealthy couple who had a big apartment here. They died a long time ago, but Emma had been here so long then, that she just stayed on. She stays in a small space, a cubbyhole, up on five. Squatter's rights, you know," he finished with a wry smile.

The same idea occurred to Joan and me at once. "Could we

meet her?" I asked.

"Oh, sure. She loves to talk, Emma does. I'll run up and get her for you," and the elevator operator disappeared behind the closing doors.

Not five minutes later, Emma herself appeared, slowly descending the stairs to our right. As we introduced ourselves, Emma held out her worn palm for a formal handshake. Her attitude was regal. I almost felt like sinking into a curtsey. I explained my interest in Christy, and she nodded, her eyes glazing in memory.

"I remember her," she said huskily. "His wife—Nancy was her name." Emma stood, both arms perched imperiously at her ample waist. "She was a lady. A real nice woman," came the words through several broken teeth. "I rode on the elevator with both of them. But I remember her because she always said 'hello'."

Joan and I were intrigued by Emma, so out of place in appearance, yet so comfortable in her memories. Warming to our approval of her performance, she began to share her knowledge of the Hotel and its history. "You want a tour of the place?" she paused to ask. "I can show you everything."

Abruptly, the night manager coughed. "Wait a minute, Emma," he interrupted her, "better not be doing that." A Scottish brogue burred his speech.

"Come on with me," Emma stated firmly, ignoring him as she turned with a stiff signal to follow her. Joan and I, a bit indecisive and yet wanting to see more of the Hotel, took several tentative steps in her direction.

"Well, don't go far," called the young manager, realizing his defeat.

Emma led us down several steps into a back hall. The area was dimly lit and dusty. Emma plowed on, carefree in her familiarity with the place. I asked what I had longed to ask, "Could we go up to Christy's floor?"

"Oh, sure." We returned the few steps to the lobby. The elevator's iron gates slid shut, and we left an incredulous night manager standing below.

"That French scarf woman lives here," Emma pointed out as we passed several floors, "and a painter named Leroy."

"Do you mean Hermes and Leroy Neiman?" I responded.

"That's right," Emma, pleased with her information, sniffed and rearranged her safety-pinned house dress, "and here's seven."

We gingerly stepped out into a deserted hall. Emma pointed toward the right, and we followed like puppies a step or two behind. At the far end of the long hall she stopped, held up a hand as would a traffic policeman and pronounced, "This is it."

A carousel of thoughts raced through my mind. "Behind this door, Christy had lived for thirty-five years," I mused. I imagined his well-dressed, often well-known clients and friends as they had also stood before the artist's doorway. Perhaps someday I'd visit Christy's abode, but not tonight.

"Now I'll show you the basement," Emma broke in. "The swimming pool is down there."

She was already marching back to the elevators. Joan and I exchanged another quizzical glance. A few moments later, we again emerged from the elevator, greeted by a large tiled expanse which boasted the Hotel's pool. An exercise room adjoined the swimming area. From its smudged-glass windows, we viewed the unmistakable designs of Leroy Neiman.

"People still swim here," said Emma. She relaxed into her own reverie while Joan and I explored the pool area. Our footsteps echoed off the old tile on the cracked walls.

"Christy loved to swim," I remembered out loud. "He was proud of his ability to navigate through even rough waters. The Muskingum River of Ohio had been his first teacher. He probably swam here often."

"Come on," Emma ordered. "There's a place upstairs I'll show you now."

Joan and I dutifully fell into line behind her. We found ourselves back in the lobby. The night manager looked up from the paperback he was reading with a relieved expression, waving briefly. Emma was already heading purposefully down the several steps toward the rear of the lobby.

We've already been down there, I thought, but there was no arguing with Emma. We stood before a closed door, one which we had not noticed before. Emma struggled to open it with gnarled hands. Joan and I, both a little skeptical about the wisdom of this particular endeavor, nevertheless pushed and shoved at the heavy door along with her. Finally, the old wood responded with a faint creaking movement. Another hard push, and we stood staring into a black emptiness. The dim hall lights afforded little help. Emma was inside the room at once. No two Girl Scouts ever followed their trusted leader down unknown trails any closer than did we behind our guide.

"Wait, Emma, stop," wailed Joan, "We can't see a thing."

My eyes gradually became adjusted to the darkness, and a few shapes began to emerge. "Where are we?" I asked. Black ropes of what must have been wiring snaked from the ceiling and coiled about the floor. Something jutted out overhead—a kind of balcony, I guessed.

"This," Emma announced with a theatrical pause, "is the ballroom!" Tickles of excitement needled through me.

"If only we could see it better," Joan broke in longingly.

"Wait a minute," Emma answered, fishing in the torn pocket of her dress. "Here!" She had rummaged up a packet of matches. Her elderly fingers trembled, but she managed to light one. The tiny flame sparked into life for several seconds revealing the vastness of the room. Joan and I followed suit immediately, lighting our own matches.

We stood there together, matches held high, surveying the aged remnants of what must have been in earlier decades an elegant setting. I knew in those moments that I would never forget the scene or the drama of the treasure discovered. I had for so long yearned to explore the hidden riches of the historic Hotel des Artistes. I could not have created a scene so vivid as this. No uniformed guide, glib with knowledge, could have provided a tour of such fascination and impact as had the bedraggled old woman named Emma.

Images rose in my mind: the seated dinners, the ceremonies, music, and dancers. I had read about the Chu Chin Chow Ball held here, the site and the setting for the first Miss America contest in 1927. Christy was the sole judge, as befitted his Barnum-like character. He and fellow-tenant, Norman Rockwell, had gone on to judge following Miss America pageants in Atlantic City, but the first had taken place here. In the brief glow of our matches I could see beautiful girls parade down red-carpeted runways.

Christy waved and bowed from the shadows.

"Be careful, Emma," Joan cautioned as the last match dimmed out.

We groped our way back to the pale light of the entrance, still following in Emma's wake. Outside in the musty hall once again, we carefully shut the heavy door. The brightness of the lobby greeted us, as did both the night manager and the elevator operator.

"Where did you go?" they both questioned at once.

"You wouldn't believe it," I answered, glancing at Joan and Emma. "It was quite a trip!"

Our last glimpse back showed Emma's sturdy form climbing the granite stairs up to her pigeonhole-home. There seemed to be a lightness, a grace, to her steps which I hadn't noticed before.

"After all," I thought, "Emma has had quite an evening herself. She's been the queen of the establishment, the unlocker of past dreams." As if she had read my thoughts, she turned toward us. I was certain that I saw the beginning of a smile move across her wrinkled face. And then she was gone.

On Saturday morning, I called Jennifer Lang, as she had suggested, for further information. She gave me two phone numbers. Ruth Peabody did not answer my ring, so I tried Olga Steckler. The phone was picked up immediately and I heard a warm and friendly response, "Olga Steckler here."

My words tumbled out. I was interested in Howard Chandler Christy. Olga said simply, "You've come to the right person. I'm called the last of the 'Christy Girls.'"

We agreed to meet at her apartment at 4 P.M. Joan had left our hotel room earlier to tour the city with family members. I wanted to see Maxfield Parrish's refurbished *Old King Cole* mural at the St. Regis Hotel. Decorated in marble, soft colors, and magnificent floral creations, the hotel offered a warm welcome. I wandered into the bar which boasted the huge Parrish painting. In contrast to the lush, cool splendor of the lobbies, the Old King Cole Room was decorated in dark, rich paneling with overstuffed seating, a comfortable haven.

I realized that I should eat something. I glanced back into the hall and saw the beautiful airy expanse of a tearoom. A piano was being played and tables were set for lunch. I could sit where I would have a fairly good view of King Cole and his merry footmen. I glanced up at the ornate chandeliers and farther up, to a ceiling frescoed with angels.

I knew that Christy had spent many evenings in the St. Regis. He attended meetings and banquets, as well as more intimate times with friends, enjoying the camaraderie and cuisine. The bar had been a gathering place for the New York writers, artists, and politicians of his day. The Starlight Roof Ballroom drew the beautiful people for more formal occasions. Christy loved the pomp and the celebration of these fancy-dress galas. Decked in black tie or white tails, he was often the center of sartorial splendor. Few could match his style.

I decided to ride the elevator up to the floor marked Ballroom, hoping it would be open this early in the day. It had been recently redecorated. I was alone in the elevator. As I stepped off, many floors upward, I could see only a vast area, almost dark, as no lights were on. The silence was engulfing. I cautiously ventured past a foyer and entered the huge room. Once inside, the room seemed to light up. The sun broke through clouds and poured in via the immense floor-to-ceiling windows. The polished hardwood floor shone as if it were illuminated. I saw a stage at the far end of the room and walked toward it, marveling at the numerous and intricate crystal chandeliers. Pink crystal teardrops fell from many-armed brass candelabras. Pink drapes framed the windows.

The Dance

It was an enchanting setting, and I was soon absorbed in pictures of the past. I envisioned the wasp-waisted women, their ballgowns billowing as they swayed to old waltzes. The turn of the century and the several decades beyond—the years graced and epitomized by the Christy Girl—came alive here as I stood enthralled in the experience. I ventured a few one-two-three steps of my own and several turns. I could hear the orchestra as it poured forth its music. Christy illustrated hundreds of such scenes: "the young debutante," "the American girl goes dancing," costume balls, and all the socially graced trappings and traditions of the age. And for these rare moments I had crossed from the wings and onto the stage.

It was time to go back to reality. Downstairs I asked the immaculately uniformed doorman for a cab. White-gloved and whistling, he was the perfect symbol of the grand old historic hotel. Outside, the noise of New York hit like a thud.

The buildings and blocks skimmed by, and suddenly we were driving through the green island of Central Park. Traffic was slower here. I could hear birds singing. Couples, arms entwined, meandered down the walkways. As we emerged from the trees, the sun once again played over the city. Here was #1, the Hotel des Artistes, and several buildings farther, Olga's home, the stately Atelier at #33.

As I got out of the cab, I looked at my watch and saw that I was fifteen minutes early. I looked up and down the street—definitely a residential block, no shops nor anything else commercial to be seen. Where to go? I began walking. The first intersecting street was filled with sidewalk cafes, flower stalls, and clothing shops. I wandered into a tiny grocery stand and bought a canned cola. Armed with it, and the resolve to be right on time, I turned to retrace my steps back on to West 67th.

A huge iced basket of pink sweetheart roses caught my eye. I immediately bought one for Olga. Roses were important to Christy. He pictured them in innumerable illustrations and paintings. Did his sister Rose have anything to do with his focus on the flower?

I entered the austere marble entry of Number 33. It was deserted. A young man came into view from the back hall area. "Can I help you?" he inquired, smiling.

"I'm here to see Olga Steckler," I said.

He nodded, "She's expecting you." The elevator, in contrast to the pristine lobby, was ancient and well-worn, adding a wonderful odd touch to the place. "You'll like Mrs. Steckler," the doorman said as we rode up. "She's a great lady." He pointed out her door.

I knocked, rose in hand. The door opened after a moment, and one of the loveliest women I had ever seen stood in welcome. An aura of friendliness surrounded her. I quickly forgot my nervousness and was drawn into a sense of ease as I followed her down the entrance hall and into her vast, high-ceilinged living room. Northern light poured in through a wall of windows—an artist's studio.

Illustrator Dean Cornwell had lived and painted here. In earlier years, Olga had been his model, and she now lived in the same setting. Her face, unlined and lovely, was framed by shoulder length red-gold hair. She wore a soft printed dress which complimented her slim figure. Slippers, in a ballet-style, graced her feet. I was enchanted by her smile and her warmth. She radiated beauty and joy. I remembered the rose and handed it to her. Beaming in appreciation, she walked into the kitchen in search of a vase.

I turned, finally aware of the room itself. The furnishings reflected Olga's warmth. The rich, dark wood of antiques, Oriental rugs, and objets d'art offered visual beauty plus practical comfort. From every wall glowed paintings and prints—a creative blending of old and new, bright and subdued. There were framed portraits, oils and pastels of scenes and faces, etchings, and lithographs.

A huge portrait on the west wall drew my attention, vibrant in color and costume, dramatic, almost flamboyant. Actor Cesar Romero sat regally perched in velvet Spanish splendor, smiling cockily as if to say, "I am Hollywood!" Olga, back with the rose in a vase, grinned and said, "Yes, it is Cesar." She answered my unspoken question with, "He's there because of a large crack in the wall. Only he was big enough to cover it completely!" I laughed at the simplicity and perfection of it.

Outside the window roof gardens blossomed; the spires and peaks of skyscrapers stretched to the horizon. To the right, Central Park beckoned a green welcome. The penthouse patios of the Hotel des Artistes seemed close enough to touch.

Olga spoke of her years in the Hotel, the glory and freedom of an earlier age. Once again I found myself transported in time. She described the relationship between artist and model: "Not like today—the click, click of the camera and then good-bye, but a close-knit, almost family feeling usually developed. We became a part of each other."

The pictures reflected this interaction. They were filled with life. "We had fun," she said. Down the halls of memory, Olga walked, talking quietly. "The special artist in my world was Rolf Armstrong." A soft smile here. "He taught me so much." She looked away, reflecting. "He's gone now. I miss him terribly." Each remembrance triggered the next, scene after scene came forth, weaving, interlocking faces, experiences, pieces of a past. We sat on a wide couch. The low table in front of us held scrapbooks with clippings and pictures.

Of Russian heritage, Olga had married an artist-photographer who later became a film director. They were divorced but remained on friendly terms. Len Steckler had recently returned to painting and she was happy for him. She spoke fondly of her parents, showing me their pictures. Her mother, now ninety-two, lived in Boston.

"Call me Penny, if you wish," she said as she turned scrapbook pages. "Rolf told me that I'd have to use a new name for myself, a catchy one which people would remember if I was going to be a famous model. I loved being 'Penny Rich.'"

Rolf had made a ukulele for Olga and taught her to hula and to sing island songs while she strummed it. There were pictures of both artist and model, the electricity between them caught by the camera's eye. Rolf was handsome, blond, dynamic. They made a smashingly attractive couple.

The cover of *Yachting* magazine appeared. Olga's jaunty attitude and a breezy sense of freedom were written in her smile. She was a calendar girl of the 1940s. She posed for many artists, from Bradshaw Crandall of *Cosmopolitan* fame to Spanish- eccentric Salvador Dali.

"What an eclectic life you've lived," I mused, "from Cesar to Salvador!"

"Oh, there are many more memories," Olga said, her eyes bright with enthusiasm.

"Tell me about Christy," I said.

"Well," she began, "I adored him. He was like a big, jolly, good-hearted and chivalrous Santa Claus. I called him that."

I listened, absorbed in her "Christy tales." I had longed to meet someone who posed for him. I remained amazed at the luck, the fate, which had brought Olga into my life. Why don't I tape this? I thought. Yet I couldn't break the spell cast by her words by reaching into my bag and pulling out a machine. So I sat, soaking up every sentence, every movement of her expressive hands, as she described her friend, Howard Chandler Christy.

She had graced a Christy poster, and I pictured the two of them, laughing and chatting, as it was brushstroked onto canvas. A print of the delightful poster appeared. The original now, sadly, was lost. It had hung for a long time in the switchboard office of the Hotel des Artistes. What had happened to it? Early posters had been mass-produced in great numbers, and many had been discarded. Original prints were rarely found, and had become highly collectible.

Olga and another Christy model, Judy Stark, had accompanied him to the dedication of the Christy Room at the Sherry-Netherlands Hotel. The three smiled in camaraderie, arms linked.

She had known James Montgomery Flagg, as well. Flagg and Christy had formed a strong bond. They became joking, hard-drinking companions as their fame grew. Flagg, too, had created posters. He unabashedly represented his own face as Uncle Sam, finger pointing: "I want you!" Olga had visited Flagg before his death. After going blind, he had succumbed to despondency, which made her heartsick.

The scrapbook pages turned. There were Pontiac ads, publicity prints for Oreo Cookies, Ritz Crackers, and Premium Saltines. Olga was the "Nabisco Girl." Posed in starched white cap and uniform, she consoled patients as a John Hancock nurse. She paused remembering another time. "I drove across the country, maybe in the late forties, and in every city there were billboards. I looked up, seeing myself pictured again and again. It was overwhelming. It felt wonderful but strange."

A *Gentleman's Quarterly* magazine lay beside the scrapbook.

Olga Steckler and some of her friends

Olga had been interviewed in an article on the "Missing Mystery Nudes" of the Café des Artistes. Intimate questions were asked about her relationship with Christy. She had been angry at this intrusion. "We were friends, period," she stated. She smiled, glancing up from the magazine, "and that's the truth."

I began explaining my own fascination with the artist. She listened with encouragement and interest. After a bit, she spoke firmly, "Helen, you have found your purpose, your life's goal. Don't ever let anyone or anything keep you from following your dream. It is your destiny."

So she understood this journey of mine.

"It's just beginning, you know," Olga continued. I sighed in agreement and with a touch of wonder.

Then I noticed that the brilliant afternoon sunlight had diffused. Pale shadows appeared. Several hours had passed. I was going to be late meeting Joan at the hotel if I didn't leave. We spent a few minutes looking over Olga's study room wall at her myriad pictorial collection of friends, so many of them celebrities.

"A cavalcade of our century," I remarked.

As I walked out of the lobby, I felt that somehow my own life had changed. I had found a new and dear friend.

That evening, high above the city, dining at the World Trade Center, I tried to reconstruct the hours with Olga, hoping to share all of it with Joan. Bits and pieces came to mind, and I leaped from one anecdote to the next. I had tried to jot notes while Olga reminisced, but I was so fascinated by her that my eyes refused to focus on pen or paper. I would have to rely on memory, and it was clouded with excitement. Each story had been embroidered with her special touch. The Dali tale was one such flashback.

Abruptly, among the many ads and poses displayed in her scrapbook, a strange picture emerged—a skull, stark and shocking in a black and white photograph. I looked closer, aided by my glasses and gasped at the realization that the "skull" was formed by six female nude bodies. Ingeniously arranged on their knees, their backsides were laced together, and their toes became the "teeth."

"What?!" Joan exclaimed, her fork suspended in mid-air.

"That's right," I continued, "it was bizarre, but unforgettable."

Olga had been one of the models, and she described the challenges of the posing process in detail.

"Wait a minute," Olga had said and left the room, returning with a large poster. When unrolled, it was the advertisement for the movie, *Silence of the Lambs*. I looked at it in confusion.

"Well?" Olga asked, waiting for my response. "Do you see the skull?" I searched vainly over the printed words and the immense moth pictured. "Here it is," she pointed out and sure enough, the skull appeared, minute but unmistakable, on the top of the winged creature.

There was more to the story. Famed photographer, Phillippe Halsman, took the original photographs, but died before the project was completed. His wife finished the work. Published in *Life* magazine, it was not well received by shocked readers. It rested in the catacombs of magazine files until resurrected by the *Lamb's* movie makers.

A perfect Paul Harvey radio sketch, I thought, as I shared the eerie finale with Joan.

On Sunday morning, Joan and I left our hotel and walked across the street to the waiting bus which would take our sightseeing group to Canada. After the whirlwind two days spent in New York City, we looked forward to the comfort of being chauffeured through the quieter countryside. I knew there would be long hours between stops and I planned to secrete myself with my new-found Christy experiences.

After meeting our traveling companions and hearing the introductory spiel given by our guide, I sat back and closed my eyes. As in the gleeful anticipation of childhood, I began to open and explore each memory, unwrapping the packages, the gifts of the past several days.

Here was Olga, welcoming and warm. I tried to recapture the wall of photographs in her study, each face with its own story, its own particular connection in her life.

Like a penny arcade, I thought, as I mentally scanned the collage. At the far left, a young actor posed for the Hollywood camera. Coffee-cream skin, huge dark eyes, turbaned, and exotically handsome, Sabu gazed out at his audience. I remembered him as the thief of Baghdad, the Elephant Boy, and Aladdin. On her own magic carpet of time, Olga reminisced that they had dated in the early years of filmdom.

The kaleidoscope turned, shifting to the next picture. Carl Sandburg, famed poet and Pulitzer prize-winning biographer of

Lincoln, stood next to, surprisingly, the queen of soapy-sexy Hollywood, Marilyn Monroe. Olga made it a threesome.

"Marilyn adored Carl," Olga spoke nonchalantly. "She even bleached her light blonde hair white in an effort to match his! I was his secretary when he was in New York."

"You knew *everyone,*" I blurted out, feeling like a star-struck school girl. There were other prints of Sandburg, one in which he strummed a guitar, singing, looking carefree with tousled hair.

A dinner scene pictured a glamorous Olga, General "Ike" Eisenhower seated a table away. In another, Eleanor Roosevelt thanked Olga's Russian folk dance troupe for their performance. Andre Segovia and Luciano Pavoratti added fame to the grouping. "He's a special friend," she pointed out with a wink, referring to Pavoratti. "Santa Claus" Christy posed also, of course, with Olga at his side. Salvador Dali, Carlos Montoya, Harold Lloyd, and other famed artists—musicians to movie stars, politicians to poets—all graced this wall.

I remembered the toast from Noel Coward's play, *Cavalcade:* "To ourselves, to each other, and to the happiness of us all." In his foreword to the Café des Artistes cookbook, Brendan Gill described so well the merry ghosts from long ago who took great pleasure in the Café experience. Surely they were present now, joining in the camaraderie of shared memories and bonded by the same wish for "happiness of us all."

I had silently invited our mutual friend, Christy, into the meeting with Olga. In Flagg's lighthearted drawing above a back table in the Café des Artistes, Christy's expression was droll, mischievous with a secret knowledge. As my quest unfolded, I often visualized that quizzical expression which Flagg had unerringly caught. Just before I turned to leave on that magical afternoon spent with Olga, I saw Christy's face, the elusive look in his eyes once again. I realized at that instant the unspoken meaning of his conspiratorial attitude. The feast was open to all. No invitation was necessary.

7

In November, Carol Ann and I returned to New York City. That timing worked for Holly, too. When Carleen and Libby heard about our proposed adventure, they wanted to come along. Each had played a special part in the Christy drama. I had first visited the Café des Artistes with Carleen some years earlier. Libby had been instrumental in contacting the Langs who owned the Café, and through Jennifer Lang, I had found Olga Steckler and Ruth Peabody. Carol Ann, of course, was my driving companion, photographer, and avid supporter. Now we, plus Holly, were to experience together whatever New York offered.

I was learning to make a few plans before these Christy trips, but to relax the scheduling as much as possible, allowing the winds of synchronicity to weave their own magic. We had definite reservations for our Café meal on Friday night at eight—that was a must. We would visit Judy Goffman on Friday morning and Susan Meyer at the Roundtable Press later in the afternoon.

We flew into the city on Thursday afternoon. Holly was to arrive on Friday morning. A chilly, steady rain greeted us when we landed at Kennedy airport. The next morning, too, was gray, with cold fog drifting about our windows. We dressed, ate breakfast, and turned up the heat. Sweatered and scarfed, we sallied out into the mist. As if by appointment, a taxi waited by the curb. Ten minutes later, the bright red door at 18 East 77th St. blinked its welcome: the Gallery of American Illustrators.

Kristin was in her downstairs office and greeted us at the ring of the bell. Jennifer Goffman, Judy's daughter, took us upstairs.

Judy, with Holly standing behind her, opened the door at Jennifer's tap. I was glad to see Holly. Her plane had landed in New York earlier than expected, a rare occurrence. Hugs and handshakes later, we were all introduced and talking.

We wandered back into Judy's bedroom. Elise's graceful nude figure was displayed in Christy style from each wall. "Are you sure this is Elise?" Judy asked Holly, pointing to one of the large canvases.

"Absolutely," Holly answered, "I'd know her anywhere." Holly shared memories and information from her background. Several hours sped by as if they were minutes. Judy glanced at her watch, "It's after one. Perhaps we'd better think about lunch. There's a good place a few blocks away."

As we walked to the restaurant, I invited Judy and her colleague Laurence Cutler to join us for dinner. Laurence was an architect and urban designer, as well as a writer. I mentioned that Olga Steckler would be there.

"Oh, yes, I know of Olga," Judy smiled. "We featured her in Rolf Armstrong's painting we had in our front window awhile back when I had the 'pin-up girl' exhibit. She heard about the show, called to say she'd love to come by and see it. But I don't think she made it."

On my first visit to Judy's gallery I had seen her showing of calendar art. I realized with a start that Olga, or Penny Rich, had been the beauty on the large easel. She had been my favorite. It was another nice connection, another interlacing of characters in the Christy drama.

The restaurant was Italian and intimate, although airy as well, with windows open to the street and hanging baskets sprouting ferns and ivies. We lunched on pasta and pizza, and good conversation.

Then Judy checked her watch with a frown. "I'm late for my appointment. Better go." She shrugged on her jacket, nodding to Holly and to me. "You two had best be going also. It's a long cab ride over to Susan's place."

Holly and I waved for a taxi. We were on our way to the offices of Roundtable Press.

We were late. There was nothing to do about it. Traffic stampeded around our cab like droves of cattle. Horns beeped and blared. The minutes ticked by, finally adding up to thirty minutes past our scheduled appointment. Our cabby missed the address given and circled the block inch by inch. Finally, there it was—the correct number stencilled above an office building. We leapfrogged out of the taxi and headed for the glass doors.

I had hoped to speak with Susan Meyer since discovering her excellent book, *America's Great Illustrators*, which was published in 1976. It had come to me in its own miraculous manner. Several years earlier, Tarran was waiting to get her hair cut. She noticed a stack of art books on the salon's coffee table and picked up the heavy, red-fabric volume on top, opening to a page headed in script with the name, Howard Chandler Christy. She asked to borrow the book, and thus I received the first in-depth published material on Christy. Now at last I had a chance to talk with the author.

"Hello, I'm Susan Meyer," stated the woman who walked toward us holding out her hand.

We followed her through a busy outer office and into a smaller one. Sunshine poured into the room via huge undraped windows. The clouds had scattered for a moment and I felt warmer, more comfortable, with the bright light.

Susan's authorship was prodigious. Rockwell and Flagg were only two of the artists she had focused upon. She had edited *American Artist* for a number of years before founding her own company, Roundtable Press.

Susan was all-business with a strong "let's get down to facts" attitude. "Why are you here?" she asked us after some minutes.

I explained that we wanted to bring out a book and film on Christy and were lining up our sources. Susan nodded in assent, mentioning Judy Goffman, Mimi Miley, and Walt Reed, author of *The Illustrator in America.*

Several light taps had sounded on her office door in the last few minutes and I knew it was time to leave. Even before the door was closed behind us, Susan had turned back toward her waiting staff. It had felt like a hurried meeting, but, in fact, it had lasted well over an hour. I was grateful she had taken the time to meet with us.

The day had passed swiftly. Twilight had fallen and the first city lights sparked on through the dusky streets. After leaving the Roundtable Press offices, we strolled for several blocks, casually window-shopping and chatting over the events of the day.

Suddenly Holly stopped and pointed to a large sign, "Look at this! Look where we are." The lettering spelled out Parsons School of Design. "This is where my mother studied," Holly stated, excitedly. "Let's go in."

We viewed a current photographic exhibit and explored the cluttered halls and classrooms. Students lounged in doorways, nodding as we passed. Holly sighed, but said nothing. I felt that she was conversing with her own memories. There were ghosts here, that was obvious from Holly's expression.

"My mother told me so much about this place," she finally said, breaking the reverie. We turned then and wandered back to the entrance. I glanced at my watch, "Maybe I'd better see about a taxi. It's after 5:30."

I glanced back at her as my taxi sped away. I had felt protective and motherly toward Holly from our first meeting. I couldn't explain it—our ages were not so diverse. But there it was. I hated to leave her alone, although her wave and "See you later!" were confident. She's an adult. She can take care of herself, I lectured myself silently but the words fell short of the feelings.

When I got back to the hotel, I found a note from Carol Ann, "Gone to the Rihga Royal [the hotel around the corner]. Be back later."

I was glad for a few minutes to myself. My mind was spinning out a replay of the day's events. What would it be like for Holly to return to the Hotel des Artistes after an absence of so many years? I was eager to meet Ruth Peabody for the first time. "Just call me from the lobby when you arrive and I'll come downstairs," she had said in a husky New England accent. Olga had promised to join us, but Susanna Fodor could not make it. I had talked with

Jennifer Lang the week before, hoping she and George might be in the city that evening, but they would be away for the weekend. Judy and Laurence assured me they would join us for drinks.

By 7:45 we four stood outside our hotel among the crowd of people waiting for cabs. Finally, it was our turn. I loved being driven through Central Park on the way to the Café. It provided a gracious, natural entrance for the Hotel.

"Almost like an overture," I thought, sentimentally. The twinkling Tivoli lights of the Tavern on the Green winked through the trees: "Lights, curtain, action!"

Olga greeted us in the lobby, looking fresh and fabulous. We walked into the Café and were immediately engulfed in the milling throng of diners.

"One member of your party is already here," announced the reservations manager after I had mentioned my name. "She's back in the bar area," he continued, "and your table will be ready in a moment." Ruth must have come down early. How would I recognize her in the mass of faces crowding the room?

We threaded our way as best we could toward the bar through the laughter and conversation. "Are you Helen?" I turned to see a woman dressed casually in wool slacks and sweater seated on a bar stool.

"Ruth!" I responded. "Glad to finally meet you."

Ruth Peabody smiled in reply, then sneezed and reached into a pocket for a handkerchief. "Sorry about that," she sniffed, "I've been in bed all day with a cold. Didn't know whether to come down or not. But here I am." Her voice was raspy with obvious discomfort.

I pressed once again through the crowd and spotted Holly, her black cape flying as she breezed through the Café door. Behind her, I saw Judy and Laurence.

"Ah, we're all here—wonderful," I thought, greeting the three.

I felt a tug at my sleeve. "We're over here," Carol Ann called out above the din. Our table, I was delighted to observe, was directly beneath Elise as the *Parrot Girl*. Perfect. Libby and Olga were seated at the far end of the table, Carol Ann next to Libby. Holly slid into the booth under her mother's lush nude figure. Conversation flowed incessantly. Words and sentences overlapped like waves on a beach. Orders for dinner were given, courses served; the waiters appeared and disappeared. The evening formed its own pattern, and that pattern was crazy-quilted with bits and pieces, scraps of thoughts, ideas and laughter—a smorgasbord of experiences, our mutual interest in Christy, and the pleasure of being brought together in the artist's milieu. I felt the thrill of conspiracy again. Christy winked from his spot on the wall, a mischievous overseer.

"This is my daughter, Gillian," Ruth announced, as a young woman joined us. Gillian had grown up in the Hotel and had wonderful stories of her own.

"If you're interested in Hotel des Artistes history, I have a great book that describes some of it," she offered. "I'll run up and get it for you," and she was up and away.

Ruth told us that she had been raised in Boston. She had always been interested in art. Her grandfather was F. C. Yohn, a fine and recognized illustrator of his day. She promised to do what she could in regard to Christy history. There were no "archives" to be researched, however. "Most of his contemporaries are gone," she added, "but I'll ask around, anyway."

Gillian returned with the book, *Upper West Side Story* by Peter Salwen. "Here you are," she smiled.

Her gift proved to be a special present. From the first page to the last, I found the book hard to put down. Peter had ingeniously incorporated folk tales, personalities, historical data, and fabulous period photographs. Tours are included, and a directory of well-known personages is in the back.

"It was a work of love for me," Peter explained later. "I had great fun with it." He had lived in the area since the 1950s. A wonderful by-product of his research was meeting his wife, Peggy, who worked at the New York Society Library.

Something caught my attention toward the back corner of our dining area, some small flurry of scraping chairs, people moving aside, faces turning, an air of the unexpected. A small man, dapper, balding, smiling, walked into the room.

"George," Olga trilled. "Over here, George!" George Lang swept onto the scene like a plump cherub, pink-cheeked and glowing.

After my second trip to New York, after speaking with Susanna Fodor and then Jennifer Lang, I wanted more than ever to learn more about the colorful figure who owned the Café. Under the hair dryer in my Dallas beauty shop, on a day not long before this New York visit, I decided to write George Lang's name on a piece of paper as I had with the Christy painting some years before. I voiced the same silent plea for "help." After all, I thought, it had worked once. It won't hurt to try. "I want to know more about George Lang."

I reached for my purse which lay on the floor by my feet. Someone had placed a magazine on top of it. I picked up the magazine and leaned to put it down on the chair beside mine. As I did so, I noticed that it was a new issue of *Town and Country*. I found my billfold, jotted down "George Lang" on a check stub, and folded the paper into a pocket of my billfold.

"That's done," I thought, "now we'll wait and see." I lifted the magazine which fell open at the contents page. A tiny color photograph caught my eye. It looked almost like— George Lang. My heart beat faster. I searched for my glasses, put them on, and looked again at the page. It was, indeed, George Lang, and an article on his newest endeavor, Gundel's, in Budapest, was featured. The finger of coincidence had touched me again. I was amazed, however, at the speed of its appearance. I should have asked sooner, I chuckled to myself, and turned pages to find the article.

Lang approached our table and Olga introduced us. What a finale to the evening. A pièce de résistance—like the Ilona torte—I thought as I reached for Lang's offered handshake. Jolly and gracious, he was a perfect host. I asked him a few questions amid the chatter. He answered each with an amusing anecdote.

At one point he glanced toward the *Parrot Girl* panel. "Bernadette Peters came in once and posed as the same girl," he said. She had been in the Café on my first visit and had sat below the drawing of Christy. I had thought then of her as a "Christy girl."

He spoke of Gundel's and his pride in that project and then about how he first knew the Hotel des Artistes. "My violin teacher lived here. I came here for lessons," he explained.

The evening had been alive with its own magic. Spontaneous and kinetic moments blended into four hours of a fascinating whole. As we wandered back into the Hotel lobby, I felt that one piece was missing: Emma.

It was late, almost midnight, but I had to try. "Do you think Emma might be awake?" I asked the night manager.

He looked up from the book he was reading with a nonchalant shrug, "Oh probably. Shall I go up and see if she'll come down?"

"Yes, please," I nodded with gratitude. He rose and headed for the stairs. A few minutes later, he was back, "She'll be here."

"It wouldn't be right to leave without seeing her," I explained to my now weary, drooping band of friends. I breathed a relieved sigh when Emma's gray head poked around the staircase corner.

"Emma! I came back!" I called out as I walked over to meet her. She looked as I had remembered her except that her dress was clean and pressed. There were no tears nor safety pins in sight.

"I know you," Emma stated with precision. "You're Helen Copley."

"Yes, that's right. Exactly right," I was surprised by her memory. Joan and I had been there over a year ago.

"Hello, Emma," said Olga, in warm greeting. "It's nice to see you again." Ruth followed suit, with a handshake of her own.

"How is your Christy research going?" asked Emma.

"Quite well," I nodded. "We've just had a splendid evening in the Café."

"I'm going to leave you now," said Ruth, her voice almost a whisper. "I'd better get back to bed." Olga joined her in resolution with a tired nod. "Me, too. It's been wonderful, but it is late. We can talk more tomorrow." Our good-byes voiced, we all made ready to leave.

I hugged Emma in farewell. "I'll be in touch. Take good care of yourself."

Her old eyes looked into mine. "I'll keep my eyes and ears open. Good luck with your Christy work." Once again, Emma had capped off the evening. The final curtain call was hers.

On Sunday morning, Holly and I returned to Judy's art-filled quarters. The round oak table was set with plates, napkins, and silver. Jennifer emerged from the tiny kitchen with a coffee pot in hand. Laurence came behind her and placed a large platter of smoked salmon, bagels, and cream cheese on the table. Judy fidgeted with a tiny black tape recorder. When the heaping plate had been emptied, the dishes cleared, and coffee cups refilled again, Jennifer punched the recorder's on switch.

Laurence was gathering material for a proposed book on Christy, to be co-authored with Judy. Thoughtful and intense, he began to question Holly. At first, her replies were somewhat stilted. She groped for answers, shifting about nervously in her chair. "The truth is," she finally managed, "I'm scared. I've never done this before."

We all nodded our encouragement. I reached for her hand and squeezed it.

The queries began again. Laurence was an intuitive interviewer. Gradually she relaxed. Her voice and composure strengthened. Her words became spontaneous, as did her memories. She spoke repeatedly of Christy's fatherly kindness and his sense of fun.

"He was always jolly," Holly remembered. "He loved playing practical jokes. Nothing was sacred if he could get a laugh out of it. He was so comfortable with being himself, he was able to tease and be teased." She related stories of his pranks and with some shyness added, "Sometimes he embarrassed me."

Then it was my turn. "How did you get interested in Christy?" Laurence asked.

"Well, it started some years ago," I began, outlining some of the events which had led to this meeting, this day. The tape rolled on, as did the hours.

When the taping session was finished, Laurence went on his way. Judy suggested a quick tour of the elegant Lotos Club. Jennifer had not been there either, so the four of us set out to explore the club's treasures.

The New York afternoon was glorious with late fall sunshine and brisk with a frosty breeze. We walked several blocks, past stately old brownstones and elegant hotel awnings. Fashionable city dwellers strolled with poodles. A typical Sunday afternoon, I supposed, as I tried to keep up with Judy's quick strides.

"Here we are," announced Judy, tripping up the stone steps to a magnificent French Renaissance facade. It was an architectural gem. She turned to glance back at us, "Isn't it wonderful? It was built in 1900 as a private home. I'll ring us in."

The inner foyer proved to be a stunning entrance, framing an intricately carved stairway. Massed fresh floral arrangements added to the decor. "There's a wedding reception scheduled for four this afternoon," the doorman explained, nodding to a huge vase filled with white gladiolas, "but you'll have time for quick tour."

Judy headed for the staircase, and we followed her to the next floor, which held a casual dining area. I fell in love with the room at first glance. It was panelled in dark wood with worn red leather and old polished brass as accents. Plaid and tweed fabrics added warmth. But the main attraction was found on the walls, which were filled side to side with framed newspaper clippings, posters, and illustrations. This was old New York in its heyday. The pictured memories came to life with startling power.

"The Little Flower," Mayor Fiorello LaGuardia, read Sunday comic strips over a crackling radio to adults as well as children during the newspaper strike; a faded newspaper account hung near the bar. Other New York mayors, governors, and various politicians were pictured beaming broadly. James Montgomery Flagg's well-known *Pirate Girl* pulled me to a another wall. The air was rich with ghosts of past figures who had lived along with Christy during the early decades of this century.

"Here's the Christy I wanted you to see," called Judy from across the room. And we looked, once again, at Elise, as intriguing and naughtily provocative as ever. The art of Gibson, Rockwell, N. C. Wyeth, and the Leyendecker brothers were there, the showgirls of Ziegfield's follies, movie stars, opera coloraturas, Babe Ruth, Will Rogers, the Roosevelts, and Al Jolson in blackface.

Lives, histories, stories, and tales of colorful events shimmered just beyond reach, yet near enough to whisper. I was captured, as I had been in Christy's old barn studio in Ohio, by the merging of past and present. I looked up at the ceiling, half expecting to see Evelyn Nesbit, "the girl on the red velvet swing," swaying to and fro. I knew that Christy had offered her respite from the bizarre murder trial—Harry Thaw was accused of killing prominent architect Stanford White in a love triangle, holding the nation's interest for months. She had accepted Christy's offer and did, indeed, flee New York City for a time to hide at The Barracks.

"We'd better go," I heard Judy's voice faintly. It was hard to come back from the daydream I had woven myself into.

That afternoon, Libby and I went to the Society of Illustrators' library and offices on East 63rd St. Holly wanted to view the Matisse exhibit at the Museum of Modern Art during the afternoon, and Carleen was lucky to grab a last-minute ticket to the *Phantom of the Opera* matinee. Carol Ann had a touch of the flu and stayed at the hotel.

Inside the Society building, the stairway was lined with framed photographs, magazines, and newspaper clippings featuring American illustrators. I was instantly caught by the faces and accounts of the early illustrators. I spotted several of the same shots Susan Meyer used in her book: Christy and Gibson dressed for a costume ball; Flagg in a contemplative pose; and a vibrantly handsome Maxfield Parrish sketching a briefly clad model. A bronze plaque boasted the names of the club's founders. Ten artists were named, one of whom was F. C. Yohn, Ruth Peabody's grandfather.

Libby was already on the second floor. "Come look at this room," she called. It was a warmly panelled dining area, its walls lined with additional striking illustrations, old and new.

After his move to the Hotel des Artistes and his marriage to Nancy, Christy turned from this art form. Portraiture became his chosen field, as did murals and the larger historical works. He ordered the burning of most, if not all, of the illustrations housed at The Barracks. It was a symbolic break, and a potent one. He never returned to illustration. Judy Goffman and Susan Meyer had both indicated that his career suffered by such a split.

The Society's exhibit-of-the-month centered on children's books. We wandered slowly along the walls lined with colorful illustrations keyed to delight youngsters. These were bold, creative, vivid works, each one different in style, light-hearted in approach but powerful as images. It gave us a chance to rediscover childhood imagination.

Walking out the front door was like surfacing from the bottom of a sea-world. Groggy with flashing colors and shifting forms, I had trouble focusing on the job at hand. We needed a cab.

We told Holly good-bye on Sunday afternoon with a sentimental farewell—high-tea in the chandelier-hung foyer of the historic Plaza Hotel across from Central Park.

"My mother brought me here when I was a little girl," Holly told us, looking about the crowded tables. We shared a pleasant hour together, and then walked out to the broad front steps to wave Holly into a waiting cab.

On Monday morning, as we enjoyed an elegant Russian Tea Room brunch, I planned out a visit to Marble Collegiate Church to see Christy's portrait of Mrs. Norman Vincent Peale.

Earlier in the year, I had called Dr. Peale's office in Pawling, New York. Christy had executed Peale's portrait sometime in the 1940s. Their professional connection led to a rich friendship. Dr. Peale referred to Christy a number of times in his sermons and books, citing the artist's worry-free attitude toward life as a prime example of his own positive thinking philosophy.

Sybil Light, Dr. Peale's secretary, told me to contact him through her for his memories of Christy. She also explained that the Christy portrait of Dr. Peale, now in the Peale home, would not hang in the church in New York until his death. "But," Sybil continued, "Mrs. Peale's portrait is hanging in the church parlor."

As had millions of others worldwide, I enjoyed Dr. Peale's many books and television appearances. I was moved by his joyful ideas, his warm and loving outlook on religion, and his relationship with God. The roots of his faith had been planted in the soil of Methodism. Although sought out by presidents, kings, and celebrities, he had never lost his genuine compassion for all people. He was a marvelous storyteller, and a witty observer of life. He was so much like Christy, I thought. No wonder they were close friends.

Several weeks after mailing my first letter to Dr. Peale, I opened the morning newspaper to the daily crossword puzzle, and began working through its maze of words. "10 across," I noticed was "Peale's appeal." Six blank spaces: SERMON. I chuckled to myself at finding Dr. Peale's name. I was growing more aware of the myriad clues in the quest that sprang up everywhere.

I can't wait to check the mail today, I thought. When I heard the click of a closing mail chute hours later, I hurried to gather up the envelopes inside. Nothing from Dr. Peale.

"Oh, well," I sighed in disappointment, "maybe tomorrow." Then the doorbell rang. I walked back to the front door, and opened it to see a postman holding out a package. "Sign here, please." The address at the top left side read, "Peale Center for Christian Living."

And so, on the day promised through my crossword message, Dr. Peale had written a warmly informative letter citing several personal memories of Christy. He had enclosed a copy of his 1984 autobiography, *The True Joy of Positive Living*. He referred to his "Christy files" and promised me subsequent memories as they surfaced. As the months passed, several more letters were sent between us.

Now the four of us stood in the foyer of Dr. Peale's church, waiting for a guide to usher us inside. A smiling, elderly man appeared in a few minutes and led us down a long, carpeted hallway where the portraits of former pastors hung.

"This is where Dr. Peale's portrait will be placed," he announced and pointed to a large open space at the end of the hall, "and this is our parlor." We entered a comfortably furnished reception room. Ruth Stafford Peale's portrait, glowing with warm light, was on a large side wall and above a long couch. Once again, the Christy style was unmistakable.

By late afternoon Carol Ann, Carleen, Libby, and I were seated in the Old King Cole Bar at the St. Regis Hotel for a last glimpse of the city en route to the airport. Some hours later, seat-belted for take-off from Kennedy Airport, my thoughts returned to the cityscape—visions of the Café, Judy's studio, Olga's apartment, the Plaza and St. Regis hotels, the Society of Illustrators quarters, and Marble Collegiate Church. The dream was real. I snuggled back contentedly into my seat and closed my eyes.

8

It was late evening when we spied the tip of the Washington Monument. Carol Ann and I had driven 1,300 miles in two days, and I had spent the previous week setting up appointments with curators and research advisors in various government agencies and museums.

We began early the next morning with the Capitol. In search of the office of the House Committee on Veterans Affairs, we explored a number of long marble hallways. Our trek ended in front of a door with stenciled gold print. From there we were escorted to the committee room by Pat Tippet, a cheerful staffer.

We had come to see Christy's portrait of Edith Nourse Rogers. Congresswoman Rogers served longer than any other representative, fulfilling eighteen terms in office. She counted among her legislative achievements the bill to establish the Women's Army Corps, sponsorship of the G.I. Bill, the Korean Veterans Benefits bill, and the bill enforcing a Nurses Corps in the Veterans Administration.

As we learned more about this charismatic woman, I could see that Christy effectively captured her strength of character as well as her feminine persona.

We had to get to the National Portrait Gallery next, so we bade good-bye to Pat and hurried via underground corridors to the central Capitol area for a quick look at Christy's famous work,

The Signing of the Constitution.

Magnificent in drama, scope, and subject, it hangs at the top of the East staircase. How could one possibly forget the impact of that moment when our country stated, as a nation, its legal principles. Christy brought the thirty-nine signers to life. He meticulously researched the project, spending months in Philadelphia at the Constitution Hall site. It was a vitally important commission for the artist, and he brought the huge endeavor to brilliant fruition. Perhaps the most highly viewed historic painting in America, Christy's work afforded great public appreciation both to the artist and to the Philadelphia experience.

Guides led shuffling crowds up and down the wide steps, stopping at the foot of the stairway to allow each visitor a chance to gaze upward into the faces portrayed.

Several tour groups marched away and another appeared. Carol Ann, practical as ever, prodded me into action. "We'd better go if we don't want to be late at the Portrait Gallery." I knew she was right, but it was hard to leave Christy's masterwork.

The Smithsonian's American Portrait Collection had been special to me since I first discovered it when we were living in Washington in the early 1960s while my husband had a job with the Department of Justice.

Carol Ann and I pushed through the side entrance doors to the gallery, only a few minutes behind schedule. The halls were lined with faces portrayed by American artists. As soon as we received our name tags and permits, we were off in search of Sue Jenkins, the gallery registrar. She was surrounded by stacks of files on her desk. A persistently ringing phone nagged at her.

Matter-of-fact, succinct, and patient, Sue demonstrated a researcher's skill with archives. She pulled out information on Christy from an immense wall of filing cabinets. Carol Ann and I pored over photocopies of Christy-related works owned by the gallery, as well as a wealth of correspondence describing these pieces. I found an unexpected bonus among the papers—a photograph of a bronze bust of the artist.

"I'll have to get permission for you to see that," Sue said. "It's in our warehouse across town."

"Please try," I urged.

"This is interesting," Carol Ann interjected. "There's a sketch of Christy by Everett Raymond Kinstler."

Sue nodded. "Oh, yes. Ray Kinstler is a great portraitist, and we are fortunate to have many of his paintings on view here."

She looked at her watch. "If we leave right now, I'll have time to show you Christy's self-portrait. It's in our basement archives. Unfortunately, the Douglas MacArthur work is off limits. It's stored in an area I can't get into."

We followed a fast-paced Sue down the hall toward an elevator. In minutes, we stood inside the vast area which housed the portraits not currently on view. As we wandered past row after row of them, faces of the past and the present looked out from various perches—a historical Who's Who on canvas.

Sue paused from time to time to point out a particular portrait or to answer our questions. In time, she stopped before the Christy *Self Portrait* which had been pulled out earlier for us. It was a powerful work, full of energy—potent with the artist's persona. His eyes were riveting, almost pulling the viewer into the artist's mind. His face was leonine, conveying a strong masculinity. A thick brush of gray-white hair capped his stern features.

"I think he looks like Vincent Price," chuckled Sue.

"I agree," answered Carol Ann, "distinguished and a little bit theatrical."

This time Christy was holding his paintbrush in his right hand, the palette in his left. "That's odd," I mused out loud. "He must have used a mirror."

"It's one of my favorite paintings," Sue said. "In fact, it hung in my own office for a long time."

I smiled at that. It was another example of the constant personal interweaving which had appeared along the way.

Sue promised to leave a call at our hotel when she arranged a visit to the Smithsonian warehouse. Then pointing us toward the library, she turned back to her loaded desk.

Cecilia Chin, the library's head of staff, met us there with a fat folder. Carol Ann and I plunged into assorted newspaper clippings, photographs, and letters. The *Washington Post* carried many write-ups, even a witty piece on "Timmie, the National Press Club Cat." Christy had painted Timmie's portrait. White whiskered and imperially posed, Timmie gazed out in feline splendor.

I was glad to see a print of Benito Mussolini's portrait there.

Howard and Nancy Christy had toured Europe in the 1930s while the artist captured members of royalty and high ranked political figures on canvas. The couple was housed and entertained in Mussolini's Italian palace for several weeks. Mussolini regarded Christy's portrait as his personal favorite, and the two men enjoyed a brief friendship before World War II.

Christy had attempted to paint Princess Marie of Rumania, but, according to Norris Schneider's files, she remained in seclusion during their visit, incapacitated by alcohol. A number of photographs I had not seen were also included. One of these was his sketch of himself as a young man, virile in a turtleneck sweater. Below it on the same magazine page, was Christy's fine portrait of John Nance Garner, Franklin Roosevelt's first vice-president.

Weeks earlier in Dallas I had tried vainly to get plugged into a constantly busy switchboard at the White House. Christy had painted many presidential portraits throughout his long lifetime, and the Christys had been guests of Calvin Coolidge during his term in office. Two presidential wives portrayed by the artist were on view there at the present time—Rachel Jackson and Grace Coolidge. I longed to see them. But, as time grew short, I wondered if I would. I packed, made other calls to D.C., and waited. Then through a last-minute quirk of fate a visit to the White House was secured.

On the day before we were to leave, Carol Ann told me to call her son Spence, who had located the right White House office to call. I dialed the number he gave me and got through at once.

"How about Wednesday morning at ten?" suggested the assistant curator.

"That's wonderful—perfect!" Once again, a gift of grace had appeared.

On Wednesday morning Carol Ann and I found our pre-assigned parking place. After our credentials were checked by the guards at a side gate entrance, we entered the reception room where Lydia Hederick met us for our Christy tour.

"Interestingly enough," Lydia said,"one of his portraits is right here in this room." She led us to Christy's Rachel Jackson. It was a small work, an expertly executed oil.

"She doesn't look like I thought she would," said Carol Ann, studying her features.

"No," I agreed. "She doesn't look like a corncob pipe smoker." A fragile lace collar framed her face, and she held a rose.

"I believe that Howard and Nancy Christy stayed at the White House at one time," I said, looking toward Lydia for confirmation.

"I imagine so," she said. "Perhaps in the Lincoln bedroom."

I told her about Nancy's love of cooking. She had gathered favorite recipes from senators, congressmen, governors, mayors, and presidents, combining them into a cookbook which she hoped to publish. When I spoke with Mimi Miley early in the Christy Quest, she mentioned that her mother, Jane Conneen, had the cookbook among the many boxes of memorabilia they gathered from the Hotel des Artistes after Bob's death.

"Nancy was eager to cook one of her special desserts for the Coolidges when she was here," I reminisced. "She supposedly sneaked down to the kitchen late one night and whipped it up."

I recalled the first time I'd seen Christy's painting of Grace Coolidge. "What is that little gold pin on her dress?" someone in our tour group had asked. Our guide told us that it was her college sorority emblem, a Pi Beta Phi pin. Later I learned that the Pi Phi national group had funded the portrait.

Lydia took us to a large room. Presidential china gleamed from sconced showcases along the walls and exhibition cases in the center. Grace Coolidge looked out serenely over the scene: she was dressed in a vivid red sheath, her dark hair simply coifed. The Coolidge white wolfhound, Rob Roy, stood by her side. The beautiful dog gazed adoringly into his mistress' face.

"I think it's one of his best portraits," I said, studying the canvas. Christy's penchant for dramatic backdrop settings was evident here. The White House glowed dream-like at the lower right corner of the work.

Coolidge had wanted his wife to be painted wearing white but Christy pushed for a red dress. He compromised by including the family's white dog.

We had gotten approval for a State Department visit and our timing worked out almost to the minute. Gail Serfaty, curator of art there, offered to see us at the only possible one-hour time slot we could manage.

The vast marbled lobby was crowded. A giant reception desk stood in the middle of the floor with people lined up around it. We chose the shortest line, hoping for a faster approach to the uniformed guard behind the desk. Fifteen minutes later, it was our turn to receive visitors badges so we could meet with Gail.

"The Hughes portrait is one of the finest paintings in our collection," she said as we left the elevator. She led us into a beautiful reception area, pointing out magnificent mahogany furniture on every side. "We're very proud of our collection of American antiques," she continued. "Our rooms are some of the most exquisite in the city. I can't take you into the main reception room today. Unfortunately it's in use."

We were in a long hallway. Portraits of U.S. statesmen lined both sides. "And here is our Christy," said Gail proudly.

Charles Evans Hughes, Chief Justice of the Supreme Court, looked out from his spot among other justices. Robed in black and painted against a dark background, only his face emerged into light. His expression was solemn as he gazed into the distance.

After many trial-and-error phone calls, at last I reached the correct office to schedule a hoped-for visit to the Washington Navy Yard. I spoke with Joe Barnes, whose cheerful voice answered my request with an affirmative. "Certainly you can visit the Sail Loft, or what we call the Band Hall," he said. We made an appointment for the following afternoon.

Joe met us with a cheerful smile. "Glad you found us." He was dressed in immaculate Navy whites. After struggling through the Washington humidity, I felt hot, disheveled and wilted in comparison.

"How about something cold to drink?" he offered, as though reading my mind. Soon we were soothed by the cold drink and cool air.

"So you're researching Christy," Joe said, taking a seat himself. "We don't have any Christy files or anything like that here, but I can show you the area where he painted *The Constitution.*"

Joe rose to escort us into the band quarters. He was an enthusiastic guide, recalling a few Christy tales of his own. "He must have been a grand guy. Lots of visitors came to watch him work. He got to know the band members and called them by name. Everyone liked him."

We entered the huge loft. Flags of each state lined the long walls, a colorful tribute to American unity. Joe pointed out the stage at the end of the room. "That's where the Navy band still rehearses and plays concerts. Sometimes we have receptions in here. In earlier years, there were fancy dress events—balls, dancing."

I had no trouble visualizing the resplendent naval officers, chivalrous and proud in gold braid and buckles.

"Right here is where they pulled up the canvas," Joe announced, pointing toward the ceiling above us. "All the men stationed here wanted to help. The canvas was incredibly heavy and unwieldy, but they finally locked it into place."

The work was twenty feet high, thirty feet long and weighed in at 1,700 pounds. Christy painted the behemoth from September 19, 1938, until the end of April 1939, working daily from nine until three.

The 290-member naval band continued its practice sessions while Christy worked, and the oompah music must have stirred his heart. He welcomed the company of the band, as well as the sailors, workmen, and congressmen who stopped by to watch his progress. He encouraged their comments, seeking their approval.

Christy's good friend, Congressman Sol Bloom of New York, had conceived the idea of the giant tableau in 1935 while working on plans for the 1937 Constitution sesquicentennial celebration. When he realized that no governmental building in Washington contained even one painting of the signing of the Constitution, he approached Christy about the project. The artist accepted the $30,000 commission with zest and thus began their joint endeavor.

Bloom and Christy researched tirelessly: faces and physical stature, individual marks of distinction, personal attitudes, clothing preferences—all facets of each Constitution signer were studied. Christy spent two years on the project, scouring libraries and museums for the figures he portrayed, as well as information about the clothing, furniture, and artifacts of the era.

When at last Christy stood before the giant canvas, he knew how almost every signer had looked in 1778. Only two of the history-makers in Philadelphia remained in question, so he made up a face for Jacob Broom and painted Thomas FitzSimons hidden behind a colleague. Christy portrayed fifty-five-year-old George Washington without his usual paunch, knowing him to have been far more active than sedentary in middle age.

To aid in the authenticity of the painting, the Smithsonian Institution lent Christy Washington's breeches, shoe buckles, and watch. From Patrick Henry's home came the pen Richard Dobbs Spaight (a North Carolina delegate) used to sign the document. And the Library of Congress offered three choice volumes from Thomas Jefferson's collection, which the artist painted into the foreground, lying stacked on the floor.

"They didn't know where to put the painting after he finished it," Joe's voice broke in. "It sat in the Capitol for over a year until they could clear a space large enough for it."

I nodded in assent. "It was actually a period of sixteen months. Finally, they moved *The Battle of Chapultepec* and hung *The Constitution* in its place, at the top of the East staircase."

The formal dedication of the painting took place on May 31, 1940. Elise's journal described the scene: It took twenty men from 8 A.M. until 4 P.M. to haul the huge painting to its temporary site on the floor of the Capitol rotunda.

"I guess it was no easier to take down the canvas than to put it up," I said, picturing the crew of sailors struggling under the weight.

"Come here," sang out Carol Ann from the far end of the room. "Here's a picture of the *Constitution* that Christy signed."

Joe and I joined her before a glass display case. "I can open that and take it out so you can read it," Joe said reaching toward a side latch. Down and along one side of the framed piece, Christy had written of his gratitude for the opportunity to paint the historic American experience and his delight in its navy-based setting.

We spent over an hour with Joe in the Band Hall, wandering from side to side of the huge room, talking and reminiscing about Christy's life and our own. When it was time to leave, I turned back for one last look. Dallas seemed a long way off in that moment. In fact, my life itself—all the years before the Christy Quest—felt distant and almost unrecognizable. I remembered how I had balked at every step in the beginning and my stubborn need to analyze each occurrence. Now, I realized how deeply ingrained the journey had become in my life. I seldom questioned anymore. I was content with the knowledge that I would continue on the path wherever the next step led.

Sue Jenkins of the National Portrait Gallery was able to track down the bust of Christy sculpted by Edgardo Simone in February 1928. We joined her at the Smithsonian warehouse surrounded by what looked like miles of stacked artifacts. We were taken straightaway to the statuary storage area. An assistant moved out the heavy bronze Christy bust for us. On a shelf with many other such works, it was tightly wrapped in cellophane sheets. Once it was unveiled, we could see the deftly sculpted visage of Howard Chandler Christy.

"Look at this," I called out, my video camera slowing as I filmed the base. "He spelled Christy's name wrong!" And there carved unmistakably were the letters, CHANLER. The D was missing. "It just makes it more interesting," I said. "One small oddity for flavor."

Friday morning offered clear blue skies for our drive to Annapolis. Christy had been a Navy man in spirit if not uniform. His World War I recruiting posters were distributed widely. His sailor girls issued a provocative call to arms: "If I were a man, I'd join the Navy" and "I want you for the Navy."

Christy's affection for the Naval Academy was deep and long-lived. His natural patriotic spirit flamed with his attachment to and work with "the Academy." Both his affection and his work were rewarded. He was named an honorary member of the graduating class of 1923 and was presented with the coveted Navy ring. Christy was the only non-graduate to ever receive this ring, and he wore it every day from its presentation until his death.

We arrived at the Academy around eleven o'clock. The campus was beautiful, as expected—stately ivy-clad buildings stood on stretches of clipped green lawns. Huge trees shaded classrooms and sidewalks. We headed for the museum.

Jim Cheevers, curator of art, and his secretary Susan had pulled out many pieces for us. We turned to the large table stacked with posters and prints. I quickly scanned the listing of Christy works

owned by the Academy which Susan had handed to me.

We began carefully unwrapping each of Christy's original works. The Sailor Girl appeared and re-appeared in many Navy "uniforms" and coquettish poses. They were delightful.

"Who were they—these early models?" I wondered. "Is Christy's first wife, Maybelle, among them?"

Maybelle remained an elusive figure in the Christy cast. The daughter of an army officer, she met and married the artist in 1899. Their years together were volatile. Their only child, a daughter named Natalie, was born in 1903. She was fought over bitterly by both her parents who separated in 1909. There were courtroom battles which eager reporters typed out into headlines. Christy brawled and drank his way through those years.

According to Norris Schneider's notes and interviews, Maybelle followed suit. I was certain that the artist had painted his beautiful wife many times, at least before the quarrels began. Mysteriously, Maybelle slipped from sight after the divorce.

In later newspaper reports, Christy spoke of his pride in Natalie's artwork. She married a Zanesville native, a tile maker named Ira Chandler, whose name was a coincidence. The couple moved in time to New York City. Schneider corresponded with Natalie and several of these letters were among his papers in Columbus. She had been displeased with newspaper comments regarding her father's alleged drinking bouts, and she mentioned that she owned none of his work. I knew that Natalie and Ira Chandler had had one child, a daughter named Carolyn.

Carolyn had also been artistic. She did not marry and remained in New York until her death in 1993. An air of melancholy, of loneliness, surrounded these members of Christy's first family.

Because Jim Cheevers had not arrived yet, Carol Ann and I decided to take a few minutes off for lunch. Susan suggested a good sandwich spot only a few blocks away, and we strode off in search of it. Halfway into grilled cheese and chips, we heard a male voice by our table. "Are you the ladies from Texas?"

We looked up in surprise. It was Jim Cheevers. He had arrived back at his office only a few minutes after we left and decided to find us to combine lunch and conversation.

I mentioned the portrait of John W. Bulkeley which I had come across from a Smithsonian listing. "Yes, we have it. It's a fine piece. It's in the museum area by my office." Jim's grin was mischievous. "You know, Bulkeley was an amazing guy. Next to his portrait, there is an artist's depiction of his PT boat. He rescued MacArthur off the island of Corregidor during World War II.

Took him out through Japanese warships. Quite a feat."

He paused and reached for a pen. "He's still living—I believe, in Maryland." He jotted down a quick note "Bulkeley."

"Maybe I could speak with him. We have one day left in Washington before we leave." That tickling sense of anticipation coincided with my words.

On the way back to the museum, we stopped at the elegant Alumni Building, where Bill Busik, alumni director, pointed out a number of framed Christy Girl prints.

At the museum again, I immediately went to find the Bulkeley portrait. It was a grand rendition of a handsome, beribboned young Navy man. In the background, warships and his famous PT boat were represented. I studied it. Christy's patriotic spirit seemed to merge with that of the officer portrayed. Strength of character and purpose were inherent in Bulkeley's pose.

Nearby was another painting. A PT boat waited at dockside while Gen. Douglas MacArthur signaled farewell to his small band of troops on Corregidor Island. Jim had told us earlier that the story of Bulkeley's rescue of MacArthur had been written by William L. White in his book, *They Were Expendable*. I had seen the movie version years before.

The artist's last portrait displayed on his easel at his death was that of MacArthur. I recalled Elise's words about Christy's affection for the general in her journal. MacArthur was Christy's first choice for president of the United States. He deeply admired the general's courage and his skill in leadership. He sent a note with a copy of a newspaper interview extolling the general to MacArthur, who responded at once. Elise had copied out his letter in her journal:

> Dear Mr. Christy:
>
> Thank you so much for your thoughtful note enclosing the clipping containing your public reference to me. I value it highly. Throughout the Pacific campaign, wherever my command post was, I never failed to have a copy of your beautiful portrait of Uncle Sam praying to Almighty God, with the inscription: "For Thine is the Kingdom and the Power and the Glory, for ever and ever, Amen." It afforded me constant inspiration along the way.
>
> Faithfully yours,
> Douglas MacArthur

I longed to see the work, Uncle Sam kneeling in prayer. It was so typical of Christy's flair for the dramatic combined with the power of spirituality. I resolved to call Admiral Bulkeley when we returned to Washington.

Back in our hotel room on Saturday evening, I eyed the message on my notepad. The words read, "Call Bulkeley." I punched in the digits. A soft female voice answered, after several rings. "I'm trying to reach Vice-Admiral John Bulkeley," I said.

"Oh, yes," came the reply. "He's right here. I'll hand him the phone."

"Fire away!" trumpeted Admiral Bulkeley from his end of the line. Startled, I almost dropped the receiver.

"Admiral Bulkeley?"

"On deck!" rang the answer.

After I introduced myself I told him I was interested in Howard Chandler Christy.

"Christy—knew him well," responded the admiral. "Did a painting of me. It's at Annapolis. But the other one is there, too." The admiral talked on, attempting to explain various facts about the other work. "D-Day Anniversary," he was saying,"Have to sign those pictures." After some minutes he paused, taking a different tack. "Alice can tell you about Christy."

Alice Bulkeley's quiet voice spoke, "How can we help you?" I explained about our trip to Annapolis and the information Jim Cheevers had given, as well as a quick overview of the Christy Quest.

"We knew both Howard and Nancy," she said. "We lived in New York City when Howard painted the admiral's portrait. We became good friends. They were wonderful people. I wanted Howard to paint our daughter also, but it just didn't work out."

Alice continued with her Christy memories, responding warmly to my questions. She explained that she and the admiral had met in China, where her British father had a business venture. It was an intriguing story, and the beginning of what proved to be a colorful and dramatic lifetime together. I remained spellbound.

My next call was to another possible Christy connection. Harry Tebbutt's name was listed on one of the Smithsonian printouts as an owner of Christy's original Teddy Roosevelt drawing. The Tebbutts were not at home, but I left a message with their answering service.

The next morning, our bags packed, we buzzed for a bellhop. Once on the main floor, Carol Ann walked outside to get our car while I checked us out. The lobby was busy. We were anxious to be on the road. I fidgeted while the people in line ahead of me checked in or out. Finally, it my was my turn.

I was putting my credit card back into my billfold when one of the hotel staffers called to me, "Helen Copley? You just had a phone call." He handed me a slip of paper with the name Harry

Tebbutt and his number. I must have been in the elevator or standing in line when his response came.

I raced out to our car, note in hand, to tell Carol Ann of the good fortune in timing.

"We've got to move," she said. "Someone's honking at us."

"Okay, but I've got to find a phone so I can call him back." Some blocks later, with no phone booth in sight, we pulled over to a curb. "It's the car phone or nothing," I said. After several rings a man answered.

"Yes, I'm Harry Tebbutt," came the pleasant reply. "And, yes, my wife and I do own Christy's *Roosevelt.*" He invited us to come by and see it after I had explained more about my Christy research.

"We're on our way back to Dallas," I replied, "but we'll take a rain check."

He explained how he had received the piece. "My father was a doctor in New York state, an eye-ear-nose and throat doctor. He treated the Roosevelt family, all of them, even Alice Roosevelt Longworth. They gave it to him in thanks for his services. When my Dad died, I inherited it."

I was fascinated. Here was a "Roosevelt connection." I had many questions but the noise from outside traffic interferred with my hearing.

"I'll have to call you back from Dallas," I said. "I'm intrigued with your story."

Harry answered,"Certainly. It's a wonderful work of art. And it presents a good picture of Teddy Roosevelt all decked out in fighting garb—the Spanish-American War period. We're very proud to have it."

"We have to come back," I said to Carol Ann. "There's no way I can miss meeting the admiral and the Tebbutts."

We had been driving for a day or so, taking it easy, not pushing to get anywhere. The pressure was off and both of us were enjoying the slower back country roads and admiring the scenery. We stopped at every "antiques" sign that looked interesting, rummaging our way through whatever old treasures lay inside.

"What do you think?" Carol Ann asked when we spotted another roadside antique mall.

"I don't know. Maybe. Hard to tell," I answered. She made a U-turn and we drove into the graveled lot. The building looked shabby, and it stood by itself in a thick grove of Georgia pines.

"How do they stay in business way out here?" I wondered aloud,"This is really the backwoods."

The building was deceptive in size, however. Once we were inside, aisles seemed to stretch out in all directions and every square inch of it was packed with the treasures of yesteryear.

"I'll take this side," Carol Ann offered, and we split up to explore. I was hoping to find some cast-iron cookware pieces for David's collection, but so far had had no luck at all. After an hour or so of browsing, I headed for the remaining few stalls on the last aisle closest to the front door. I had seen nothing of interest. You'd think that out of this mass of stuff, there'd be just one Griswold skillet, I thought.

Then I glimpsed something small and black and wandered back toward it. It turned out to be a tiny replica of an old cooking stove. It was in good condition and all its parts were intact, even to the miniature pots and pans resting on its surface. I was thrilled. Finally, I had something to bring to David. I picked it up carefully. I wasn't an expert on old iron, but this piece just felt right.

I was turning to walk out of the booth with the stove when I glanced to the wall directly above. Several framed pictures hung there. My skin sparked with electricity. I bent forward for a closer look. "It's Uncle Sam, it's Uncle Sam kneeling in prayer," ran the mental switchboard inside my head. "It's Christy's poster of Uncle Sam! It's a print of the poster!"

When we were at Pearl Harbor earlier in the quest, David and I found a book about World War II. Thumbing through it, I paused at a page of war posters. Here was Christy's Uncle Sam. Above his figure, large letters spelled out "Faith of Our Fathers." Below, in smaller print, were the words,"For Thine is the kingdom and the power and the glory." Scenes of wartime blended into the background. I bought the book and had studied the small picture many times.

The hope of finding a print of this poster had been in my mind since then, but it had eluded me until today. I reached for it eagerly and only then did I glance at the piece beside it. It was a picture of Gen. Douglas MacArthur. His piercing eyes seemed to be gazing directly at Christy's poster. I took both pictures from the wall.

"Carol Ann, come quick," I bellowed. "Hurry!"

I watched her astonished expression with glee. "I still can't believe it," I said. "The stove pointed to the Christy poster and MacArthur. And to find the two side-by-side—what are the odds of that?"

"What if we hadn't stopped here?" I asked Carol Ann as we got back into the car.

"But we *did* stop," she answered patiently. "And you did find your miracle."

A gentle Georgia mist fell during the third day of our trip. We were scoping out an afternoon route as we lunched at a roadside cafe.

"We're close to Athens," I suggested. "I've never seen the University of Georgia. As I remember, their museum owns a Christy. What do you think about a quick visit?" I rooted out the National Portrait Gallery list one more time. I had not called the Georgia museum beforehand for information because I didn't know the direction our path home would take.

"Why not?" answered Carol Ann. "We've had good luck so far."

Spreading magnolia trees dotted the lawns of white-columned homes in Athens. People seemed to have "take it easy" written in their faces.

We found the campus gates after making a few inquiries to pedestrians on street corners. Once inside the university complex, we drove in circles until at last we spotted the ivy-covered art museum. It had begun to rain harder.

"I'll go in and see if their curator is in. This is so last-minute and slap-dash, it may turn out to be nothing. No point in getting you wet, too."

I didn't expect much from this visit. From past experience, I knew that curators preferred specific appointments. Their time was at a premium and they were often bombarded with requests from art patrons. Still, it was worth a try.

I asked the young aide if the gallery owned the Christy nude which was listed on the Smithsonian printout. She did not recognize the name of the piece, but pulled out a catalogue. "Here," she smiled, looking up at me,"it's in our archives, in storage. You'll have to get permission to see it."

A tingly prickle began at the back of my neck. There was "something" here, and I knew it was important.

"The curator may not be in her office today," the aide continued. "Let me check." I fidgeted nervously while she spoke with several secretaries. "Okay, thanks. I'll let her know," she finally said into the phone. I had my fingers crossed on both hands.

"Ms. Mondi will be back in a few minutes. She's the curator and you can wait in her office," the aide stated. "I'll show you how to get there."

I thanked her quickly and turned to go back outside. "Carol Ann! Pay dirt!" I yelled from the museum steps. "Come on."

A few minutes later, we were ushered into a bank of offices, each separated by frosted plate glass dividers. It was not a long wait. Annelies Mondi appeared, raincoated and damp, to greet us. I liked her at once.

"Did you see it, the Christy nude?" she asked after we had introduced ourselves.

"No," I answered, puzzled. "Where is it?"

"Right here on my wall," she pointed to a very small oil painting on the wall inside the adjoining cubicle. In fact, I realized, it was the smallest Christy work I had ever seen.

"When I heard that you were interested in Howard Chandler Christy, I was intrigued," Annelies said, "since I have his painting in my own office."

The nude stood full-length against an indistinct background. Her head was bowed, as if in prayer.

"The girl at the information desk said it was in your archives," I said. "It's a nice surprise to see it here, so easily accessible."

Annelies smiled. "Then you have another surprise coming. We also own a Christy portrait and it is in the storage area. We can pull it out for you."

I glanced at Carol Ann, who looked back at me quizzically. Serendipity had again touched our trip with this unexpected bonus. We followed Annelies through museum halls and down a back stairwell.

"Let's see now," Annelies said, looking down the numerous

rows of precisely stacked paintings. "I believe it's just about here." She reached into a group of very large framed works. "It's heavy.

She found a helper and they gingerly pulled and tugged together until the portrait emerged. They carried the painting to an easel and stepped back.

My breath caught. A young woman sat serenely looking out at us.

"She's beautiful, isn't she?" Annelies whispered. I nodded in agreement, but I couldn't frame words to express what I saw in the girl's face.

"Her eyes," I ventured,"There is something, well, *more* in her eyes." I turned to Annelies. "Who is she?"

Annelies shrugged. "I don't know. And there's nothing written on the back to give us a clue."

Only the artist's signature was visible. Here was another mystery. "It's as if she knows something we don't know. Almost as if she's trying to tell us something."

"I believe we may have a folder on Christy,"Annelies said thoughtfully. "The information may be there."

I took one last long look at the portrait. I would not forget her exquisite face nor the aura of mystery inherent in the portrait. I had been touched in a way which I knew would remain with me.

When we reached the file room, Annelies found the Christy folder. I eyed it with pleasure. Annelies thumbed through the sheets. "There are a lot of letters in here. And here's the write-up on the portrait!" She seemed to have caught the spirit of questing herself, as she laid out the folder for our inspection.

Carol Ann picked up several papers. "These are original letters," she said with wonder.

I was busy reading the background data on Christy's work and barely heard her. I was beginning to understand the strange light in the girl's eyes. Christy had painted her posthumously. Her parents had summoned the artist to render a lasting tribute to their only child who had died a year earlier. Her name was Ethelyn Talbott.

The three Talbotts were returning to the United States from a stopover in China. They must have been elated at the prospect of coming home after U. S. Army Colonel Samuel Talbott's tour of duty in the Philippines. Adding to their pleasure, their daughter had met a young Air Force captain, A. W. Kissner, also stationed in Manila, whom she planned to marry. Then, an unexpected tragedy struck. Ethelyn died of scarlet fever on board ship, several days after their departure. Ethelyn's fiancé had left his post in the

Portrait of Miss Ethelyn Sarratt Talbott, 1938

Philippines some months earlier.

Talbott was descended from the prestigious Calvert family of Lord Baltimore, which had been instrumental in founding the state of Maryland. Through inheritance he had received land situated next to Mount Vernon on the Virginia waterways. Their home, long known as "Ferry Landing on the Potomac," had been constructed there.

Colonel Talbott died in 1965 and was buried along with his daughter in the family plot at Arlington National Cemetery. When Mrs. Ethel Talbott died in 1970, Ethelyn's portrait was passed on to Kissner. The museum at the University of Georgia received the painting as a gift from then Major General Kissner, who donated the work in memory of Colonel Talbott.

Carol Ann handed me a stack of letters, and I gave her the background sheet. I felt that we had stumbled onto a real find—here were Christy's words, page after page of them in his scrawling handwriting. The eight letters gave us insights into his creativity. Christy, the artist, spoke to his patrons with the compassion of Christy, the man. The painting which emerged from his desire to portray the girl's spirit was a tribute both to his talent and her innate beauty.

I was curious to see the FDR retreat at Warm Springs, Georgia, where he died. The Little White House is located in a beautiful spot among rolling hills covered with pines. We reached the grounds on a crisp, almost cool, morning which welcomed us with blue skies.

Christy produced four presidential birthday portraits for Roosevelt. Each had been printed and distributed as posters. One original oil hung here in Warm Springs. We found it quickly. Here, again, was Elise posed as the Spirit of America, clad in almost translucent fabric. Several children were portrayed, their young faces turned upward toward their president.

The piece was under Plexiglas and I struggled to capture it on film without a glare. I also videotaped it, dodging between tourists. I now had four excerpts on the video reel: Annapolis, the Navy Sail Loft, the Smithsonian warehouse with Simone's bronze bust of Christy, and this one from Warm Springs. I was learning to use the equipment and that felt good.

Carol Ann and I continued our tour of Roosevelt's retreat, enjoying the picturesque setting and the historical feel of the place. I breathed in the clear, pine-scented air and wondered if Christy had wandered these grounds himself. He would have relished the rural atmosphere. Visitors of all ages and from many countries were here today. He would have liked that, too. I could almost hear his hearty laugh and see his outstretched hand greeting each person.

Birds circled and chattered among the sentinel evergreens. High overhead a single jet sped across the sky. I sensed a kind of benediction for our trip. We crossed the parking lot, climbed back in the car, and turned toward Texas.

9

I planned a second trip to Christy's bucolic spread in Duncan Falls, Ohio, for late summer of 1993. I knew that Polly Pedjoe would be visiting her Ohio family in September, and I wanted her to join us.

I first came across Polly's name when I went through Norris Schneider's voluminous data on Christy. He had included Polly's letter of inquiry regarding a Christy art show held in Ohio in the 1970s. She later sent several Christy pieces from her own collection for the showing. Her letter spoke enthusiastically of her interest in the artist. Her aunt (her mother's sister) had married Christy's only brother, Bernard. Unfortunately, there was no return address on her letterhead.

"Someday, somehow, I'll find Polly," I resolved. Later, Mimi Miley mentioned someone who had at one time contacted her about Christy—"a lady from California who's a Christy relative." Could it be Polly? I kept hoping for a clue as to her whereabouts but none came. When I placed ads requesting information on the artist in several newspapers, a number of letters arrived in response, but there was nothing from Polly.

Then one day a letter did appear from Mrs. Polly Pedjoe. I tore it open and scanned it quickly. She said that she had heard of my interest in Christy, offering a bit of her Christy background. She closed with "Please let me hear from you." I called her immediately and we talked for more than an hour, sharing pieces of our lives, as well as our mutual fascination with the artist.

Polly was my age with a retired Air Force husband and three grown children. It happened again—that sense of having always known someone. When we ended the conversation, I was sure that I'd discovered a special friendship. Synchronicity, or what I now called grace, had occurred once more.

Polly had heard about me from a high school classmate she had reconnected with while in Zanesville at a reunion. Some months later, the friend called Polly saying that a mutual friend had spotted my ad in the Sunday edition of the Zanesville newspaper. It was odd, the friend recalled, that she turned to the ad pages at all. It was something she never did. The name "Christy" caught her attention and she thought of Polly.

She said my interest in Christy was "a miracle." I had to agree with that. Several months later David and I flew to San Diego to visit the Pedjoes, who lived in a beautiful semi-tropical coastal town. Four lovely days later, we departed with new Christy knowledge and a firm friendship with Polly and "Pedj." I realized I'd again met someone who would share my enthusiasm with the Christy Quest and whatever miracles lay ahead.

As I began assembling a group to tour The Barracks, Holly was number one on the list. She had never been to her father's country home. I also wanted to include Polly's cousin, Annette Trembly of Columbus, and local Christy enthusiasts. I made lunch reservations for twenty at the Zanesville Holiday Inn and kept my fingers crossed that we'd have a good turnout. Tom and Barb Hayes generously agreed to open their home and grounds to us after lunch.

Saturday dawned with chilly rain, but I scarcely noticed. Our group totaled fifteen when we were ushered into the Holiday Inn dining room. We were a mixed bag: Polly's brother and sister-in-law had come from their home in Arizona; Dr. & Mrs. Gordon Gifford of Zanesville (Dr. Gifford's dermatology clinic displayed many Christy pieces); Vivian Glenn of the Morgan County Historical Society; the Hayes relatives; and, of course, Holly and Jim.

We shared Christy stories for an hour and a half, then headed for the farm. Amazingly, each car in our entourage rounded the last bend in the gravel road by 2:15, within fifteen minutes of our scheduled arrival—and there it was, grayed by time and the steady rain: Christy's beloved Barracks. The weathered red barn still stood as a silent sentinel.

Umbrellas raised, we sloshed up to the front porch. We were rather a bedraggled bunch, but eager to explore. Barb and Tom

The barn at The Barracks

ushered us into the house, taking jackets, slickers, and umbrellas. The Hayes children and dogs skirted about us as introductions were made. Then we wandered and browsed through the place for some time, ending up around the dining room table.

From the head of the table, Tom answered our questions patiently. Holly added her personal insights. I watched her face; a range of emotions played across her features. I sensed what must have been conflicting feelings welling within her. It must have been hard to present herself as Christy's daughter to family members she'd never met, but she carried it off well.

The rain continued, but we resolutely donned raincoats again for a walk to the studio. Up the dark, narrow steps we climbed slowly, one by one emerging into the larger but much brighter second floor. I made a beeline to the wall stacked with family odds and ends—sports equipment no longer in use, children's discarded toys, and frayed holiday decorations.

The blue model's platform was buried beneath numerous boxes and crates. I'd dreamed of standing on it with Holly beside me since I first spotted it. With Tom's permission, we set to work clearing it off.

Freed of its load, it stood on rusty rollers, a mute witness to a time gone by. I stepped up onto the platform carefully. Holly was a bit reluctant, and she had to be coaxed. For me this was a very special moment. My sentimental request fulfilled, I stepped down, gratified. I could hear the rain outside and the voices buzzing about the loft, but I felt closed into a pocket of inner silence. Christy's presence seemed real in that space. Then with a shrug, I came back to the present. The blue platform was again stowed against the barn wall, and our group inched down the creaky steps.

Outside, we bade a rainy farewell to Holly and Jim, thanked Tom and Barb for their hospitality, climbed into our cars and began a slow descent to the road.

My mind brimmed with a whole new set of questions. Every adventure along the Christy journey had brought forth, not only people, places, and events to be explored, but an ever-deepening personal dedication to the quest itself. I did not doubt the power of Christy's spiritual energy, for it had brought us together from Ohio, California, Texas, Indiana, and Arizona. We'd come back to the home he had built and loved and so, it seemed, had he.

By September I had collected enough frequent-flyer mileage to travel free to New York City. Polly Pedjoe and Annette Trembly planned to meet Carol Ann and me there for a weekend.

Several weeks before our departure date, I began to plan the trip. An evening in the Café was always a must, and there were a number of Christy friends to see. Each visit added new contacts, and I was curious to find out who would enter the stage in this act.

Musing over the upcoming trip, I sat with pen and paper before me. I had made reservations for eight at the Café des Artistes. That was done. Now what? Suddenly a name printed out in my mind. Each letter was in exact detail. Looking up, I could see the name with clarity, with my "physical" eyesight. I didn't recognize the name for a minute or so: Everett Raymond Kinstler. I shook my head and wrote the name on the yellow pad in my lap. An indistinct memory tugged. I tried to clear my mind and asked for help.

"An artist," I thought, "He's an artist." As a stab of recognition hit, I scrambled for my Washington notes made the year before. There, from Sue Jenkins' listing was Kinstler's name. He had done a sketch of Christy. "Am I to contact him?" I wondered with amazement. The printed sheet gave no further information on Kinstler, only the description of his drawing. I thought back to another time eight years before; the same thing had happened when I was given the name, "Gamaliel."

"Well, okay," I reasoned, "I asked for help that time and I waited, believing I'd get understanding, and I did. So, I'll trust again."

I had errands to run and was busy until late afternoon. When I came back home, I glanced at the pad on my bedside table. "Kinstler" was written across one line and a question mark beside it. I unloaded my grocery sacks and walked up to the mail slot. There was a letter from the National Portrait Gallery. I tore it open immediately. It was from Joan Stahl, curator for the Juley Collection there. I had missed meeting her when Carol Ann and I visited Washington on the first research trip. She had sent a listing of the photographs from their Christy collection. Peter Juley and his son had gathered 400 photographs of the artist's work and of the artist himself.

I began reading Joan's letter with interest. She had been to New York, returning to Washington the day before. In New York she had met a highly respected portraitist. She happened to think about my interest in Christy when he mentioned his tutelage under James Montgomery Flagg. The artist's name, Joan continued, was Everett Raymond Kinstler. I read the name over and over.

"Mr. Kinstler knew Howard Chandler Christy and would be glad to talk with you if you wish," the letter continued. And there was his address and phone number.

Joan had added that Kinstler was at the height of his career, a vibrant man. Several of his presidential portraits were hanging in the White House.

It was 5 P.M. Dallas time, therefore 6 P.M. in New York. I wrangled with my doubts for fifteen minutes or so. I knew I'd lose courage if I tried writing out questions or thinking about what to say. I picked up the telephone. It rang several times, then a recording came on.

I left my name, phone number, and a message about my interest in Christy. Then, almost relieved, I hung up. Well, I thought, I tried. I did not expect a return call. Everett Raymond Kinstler was a renowned artist, far too busy for odd calls like mine. I'll just write to him, I resolved, then I can take some time and do it right.

I got up and sorted through the rest of the mail. I was writing out a few checks when the phone rang. In my determination to finish my bookkeeping task, I almost ignored it. But, sighing at the distraction, I reached for the receiver.

"Hello. Is this Helen Copley?"

"Yes, it is," I answered, thinking ruefully that I'd been caught by a salesman.

"This is Ray Kinstler." Shock hit me for the second time that day. I scooped up a pen and the yellow notepad. "Mr. Kinstler! Thank you for calling back!"

"No problem," he responded, "and call me Ray. I have a few minutes to talk. I have a high regard for Mr. Christy's work and I knew him slightly." He went on to describe several visits with the artist—once, in Christy's studio at the Hotel des Artistes and a chance meeting in Central Park. "It was just before he died. It was winter. Snow on the ground. Cold. Mr. Christy was striding along out there—no overcoat on. We talked for a few minutes."

Ray also shared some of his own background, his close friendship with Flagg (Monty), and his career as a portraitist. I was fascinated by his description of New York in that age of famous illustrators. He knew the city and its artists intimately.

He spoke of his book, *Painting Portraits,* which Susan Meyer had edited. I told him about Holly. He was intrigued by my quick sketch of how Holly and I had met. He had to get to another appointment then, but said, "I want to talk longer with you about all this. I'll try to call you back later. I've really enjoyed our visit. It brings back so many memories. I'll be in touch."

I looked down at my notes. "Did this really happen?" I questioned. I'd made an earlier notation to call Olga. I punched in her number and was answered by "Olga Steckler here."

"Olga, I'm coming to New York in two weeks," I told her. "We'll have another Café evening."

"That's wonderful," she answered. "Tell me what's been happening on the Christy Quest."

"I just had another miracle," I said."I talked to an artist who knew Christy. His name is Everett Raymond Kinstler."

Olga was silent for a moment and then shot back, "Ray Kinstler. You spoke with Ray Kinstler?"

"Yes." I rambled on, describing the conversation.

"Helen," Olga said with authority, "Ray Kinstler is probably the most sought-after portraitist in the country. Everyone adores him. He has a fabulous studio in the National Arts Club." She paused, obviously trying to frame her next words, "How did you reach him? How—?" Her question trailed off.

I explained what had occurred in the afternoon, ending with, "So I just prayed for courage and telephoned his number. And I got his answering machine. Then he called me back."

"Well," Olga stated, "That's really something. He's so busy. I'd say you did have a miracle. But that's normal for you—your story is all about miracles."

After Olga hung up, I decided to call Polly in California. But as I reached for the telephone, it rang.

"Helen, it's Ray Kinstler. Do you have time to talk?" Indeed I did and I again grabbed up my yellow pad. An hour passed swiftly. Ray was a warm and witty man, exceedingly knowledgeable, bright, and intuitive. I was having a glorious time listening to his experiences. Curious about my interest in Christy as well, Ray invited Carol Ann and me to visit him in his studio quarters at the National Arts Club. He had lived there since its opening, the first artist to move in. Christy had been the first apartment owner at the Hotel des Artistes. It was another interesting coincidence.

When we signed off, I took a deep breath and asked if he might join us for an evening at the Café. He answered in the affirmative, and I was thrilled. He promised to send a copy of his sketch of Christy. "Stay in touch," he said, "Call me when you get to New York."

After I put down the phone, I went back over my notes, adding everything I could remember from the conversation. At the bottom of the page, I wrote in big capital letters: "I'VE FOUND A NEW FRIEND!"

Fifteen minutes later I picked up the phone to hear Ray say, "I forgot to get your address!" We laughed at the joint oversight. I was too excited to sleep much that night. I kept visualizing the New York scenes and people Ray had described. I looked forward to reading his book on portraits. More than that, however, I wanted to meet my new found Christy shipmate in person.

Weeks later, Carol Ann and I checked into the Salisbury Hotel on West 57th St., just down the block from Carnegie Hall. After unpacking and settling in, I called Olga. Polly and Annette hadn't arrived.

I reached for the pad with Ray's name on it. I'd promised to call him as soon as we arrived. He picked up the phone right away, welcoming us to the city. He would meet us at the Café on Friday evening. We could set up a time to tour the National Arts Club and his studio-quarters during dinner.

Next I telephoned Ruth Peabody. "What would be the possibility of seeing Fannie Hurst's apartment?"

She sighed. "Not much chance. It's on the market and the artist who lives there is hard to contact."

I plunged ahead. "Can you try? I feel so strongly that we're to go there."

She answered without much enthusiasm, "I'll be glad to. But don't get your hopes up."

I turned to Carol Ann. "We're on hold with Fannie."

She grinned. "Ten to one it'll come through. "

Fannie Hurst was America's premier sob sister, one of the best to write what would later be called "soap operas." Several of her most popular novels were made into movies. Lana Turner suffered through one dramatic trauma after another in *Imitation of Life;* Susan Hayward and John Gavin loved and lost in the 1961 version of *Back Street* (which was filmed three times). Fannie wrote *Lummox* in 1923; she considered it her best work. *Humoresque,* a collection of short stories, was also filmed with much success.

I had reached for Kleenex along with other moviegoers in the 1950s and 1960s. My first encounter with Fannie Hurst had occurred on a movie screen; my second at the foot of a banyan tree in Hawaii.

Fannie was born in Ohio (as were Christy and Dr. Norman Vincent Peale) in October 1889. Her death came on February 23, 1968. I could not meet her in person, but I knew that somehow, in some way, she would help me. I resolved to find her autobiography, *Anatomy of Me,* now out-of-print. Other "Fannie clues" soon began to spring up.

While shopping for a gift in my neighborhood bookstore, my glance fell on an arresting female profile which graced the cover of The Literary World Calendar. Sure enough, it was a youthful Fannie Hurst. From the write-up inside, I learned that Fannie had been an early advocate of women's rights and an outspoken champion of the downtrodden, the "underdogs" of the world.

These less fortunate figures peopled her novels, coming to life under her pen, as did the faces on Christy canvases. But Fannie's characters had an added dimension—their author lived out the scenarios in her own life. She became a chamber maid, ironing her way through stacks of wrinkled garments. When travelling to Europe, she booked her passage in steerage. In her "real" life, Fannie was very wealthy, but her heart lay with those who struggled to make a living. She moved into the exclusive Hotel des Artistes in 1932 and lived there until her death.

From a serendipitous meeting with Betty Ruth Fogelman, a docent at the Gilcrease Museum in Tulsa, I learned that she had spent a summer in residence at the Hotel des Artistes. Her father rented an apartment there for several years during World War II. Betty Ruth, a young girl at the time, arrived by train from Tulsa on V-J Day. She described the excitement of the throngs gathered on the city streets, the colorful parades, all the glory and pomp expressed on the historic occasion.

Betty Ruth met Nancy Christy several times at the Hotel, but not her renowned artist husband. I listened to her reminisce, trying to recreate the Hotel scenes in my own mind.

Then, as we were voicing our good-byes, she said, "There's something else. An apartment there always intrigued me. I think—no, I'm sure—a woman writer lived there. It was on my father's floor, just down from his place. I always wanted to meet her. Her front door was magnificent—made from beautiful wood. I heard other residents talking about how large and fabulously furnished her apartment was. She traveled a lot, and was gone that whole summer. I can't remember her name. . . ."

I grinned. "Was it Fannie Hurst?"

Betty Ruth's eyes lit up in recognition. "Yes! Yes, it *was* Fannie Hurst. How did you know?"

I told her about Fannie's tree in Hawaii. She clapped her hands and said mischievously, "Maybe her front door was made from banyan wood!" We laughed at the thought.

She continued, "All I know is that I spent what seemed like hours standing in the hall staring at her door, praying it would open and I could peek inside."

In the following months, I lingered over our conversation many times. While I scouted for information on Fannie in libraries and bookstores, another possible source came to me—Olga. My intuition proved correct.

"Oh, *Fannie.*" Olga's musical voice sang out over the telephone line, "I knew her well. Very well. In fact, I typed several manuscripts for her."

"Tell me everything," I urged.

"She had two tiny dogs. She walked them every day, up and down the block," Olga remembered. "And she lived in the biggest apartment in the des Artistes. Another woman lives there now. An artist. She redecorated Fannie's place—it's totally different now."

Olga described the old-world beauty of Fannie's furnishings, stating that she had filled her home with treasures gathered in Europe. "Fannie even had a lovely old Gothic dining room dismantled and reassembled in her apartment. It was a wonderful spot. There was also a small chapel-like room with stained glass windows on the third level of her apartment. It was where she wrote." Olga talked on, pulling me into a visualization of the elegance of an earlier time.

"How I'd love to see it," I mused, "no matter how much it has been changed."

Olga paused. "I suppose it's possible, but it won't be easy."

I thought of Ruth Peabody, "Maybe Ruth knows the artist living there now. I'll ask her."

Now, on a bright Friday morning, it was time to call Ruth again. "I did reach the owner of Fannie Hurst's apartment," she said, "She's terribly busy, but you can call her. And keep your fingers crossed."

I immediately dialed Valerie Markwood's number. She was polite, but obviously under pressure for time. "If you can be here at four sharp, my assistant will tour you through," she said.

I agreed, excitement bubbling in my heart.

Olga led me to another connection, the world-famous photographer Arnold Newman. She told Arnold and his wife, Augusta, what I was doing, and gave me their home number.

Mr. Newman answered the phone himself. He was quite cordial, saying that he would be in his studio in the afternoon and would set aside a few minutes to talk with me. I was elated.

By two that afternoon, we were climbing the stairs to the art gallery where we were to rendezvous with Polly and Annette. The gallery door was opened by the owner, a tall man with a rather serious demeanor. I heard female voices beyond and rushed past him for hello hugs. Just over Polly's shoulder I spied the original oil painting of Christy's popular poster, *Americans All*. As I turned to call Carol Ann's attention to it, I looked into a large side wall of the gallery. I was speechless. A huge work in oil hung there—the splendid rendition by the artist of Uncle Sam kneeling in prayer.

I exploded with joy. What a gracious gift! The timing and setting were totally unexpected, yet perfect.

By the time we left the gallery, I was worn out by the emotional impact of the experience. I felt like a rag doll. The gallery was located at the top of a long series of dimly lit steps. I took one stair step down, slipped, and plunged forward. I sat in an ungraceful heap as Carol Ann, Polly, and Annette came to my aid. My back hurt, my knees hurt, but my pride was more deeply injured.

"I'm okay—I think," I peeped, answering their concerns.

"Let's just sit here a few minutes," suggested Polly. I nodded gratefully.

"I've heard of show-stopping entrances," said Carol Ann, "but what an exit!"

It felt good to relax for a moment. Then I remembered the promised telephone call to Arnold Newman. I didn't want to miss that connection.

"Do I dare tackle those stairs again?" I asked, "The gallery telephone is probably our best bet." Up I rose, still somewhat shaky from my pell mell descent. Returning to the gallery, I called Newman's number. A busy signal. I groaned in disappointment. While I waited to place the second call, my mind returned to the first mention of Arnold Newman's name in connection with Christy.

I knew that Newman's work ranked with that of Karsh, Beaton, Avedon—the finest portrait photographers. He worked in black-and-white prints and had produced several classic books.

The artist's genius for capturing each subject's character was obvious. Every portrait made an indelible and powerful impression. Like Christy, Arnold Newman had left a cavalcade of famous faces, the history-makers of the twentieth century.

I took a deep breath and dialed again. This time, as before, Newman answered himself. He was in the middle of being filmed for a television program, but he thought this was a good time to take a short break. He talked easily about the history of the Hotel des Artistes. He knew the famous Café-goers and Hotel residents and had photographed West 67th St. through the last four decades.

"I'll be glad to help you in any way I can," he offered. I blurted out an invitation for dinner at the Café that evening.

"Well," he answered, "let me speak to Gus about it. We were there only last night. We have guests due in for the weekend. And she might have something else planned. Call back a little later."

I hung up and sat fidgeting while my watch ticked out slow minutes. Eternities later, I dialed again. "We'd be happy to come," stated Mr. Newman. "Gus says she can't turn down another chance for her favorite cheesecake."

I stood before Christy's *Uncle Sam* painting for one last long look. "Thank you," I whispered, and turned to rejoin my three waiting friends on the steps below.

"Look at the time," said Carol Ann. "Aren't we due at the Hotel at four?" It was 3:45. We pulled to our feet and started off in search of a taxi. At 4:05 P.M. we were deposited at #1 West 67th Street.

"Cross your fingers," I whispered and pressed the bell. The front door itself was a masterpiece. As Betty Ruth Fogelman recalled, the wood was beautifully carved. After a moment the door opened, and we were greeted by a diminutive young woman.

"You are Helen Copley?" she questioned in a voice touched with foreign flavor. Her eyes quickly passed over each of us.

"Yes," I nodded, "And these are my friends. Thank you so much for seeing us. " She introduced herself as Ms. Markwood's assistant, turning immediately with a gesture to follow her.

From the foyer we walked into the most beautiful artist's studio I had ever seen, either in person or in illustration. Late afternoon sunlight poured into the great room from a wall of windows. The ceiling rose two and a half floors upward. We stood awed by the sheer size of the place. As if by rote, I unearthed my small camera.

"No pictures," our guide admonished. We collectively sighed in disappointment. "Who could forget this anyway?" I whispered to Polly.

A long rectangular work table occupied the center of the studio. Neatly stacked brushes and hundreds of paint tubes lay on the tabletop. Many canvases stood on easels or were stacked against walls, each making a bold statement in the genre of modern art.

"We haven't much time," stated our guide. "I must leave in

twenty minutes." We nodded like chastised schoolgirls and followed her into the next room. Here I sensed a whiff of Hurst atmosphere. Leaded glass windows had been retained. Paneled in dark wood, rather than the whitewashed walls of the studio, it offered an old-fashioned charm.

"This is the kitchen," Ms. Markwood's determined aide announced from the next doorway. On we went, filing meekly past her. As our tour progressed, I began to understand her determined pace. This was a huge apartment. On three levels, bedroom after bedroom appeared. The room I longed to see, however, was Fannie's chapel. She had imported it in its entirety from Italy. I hoped it had been left intact. And so it had. It was the last room we visited.

The wonderful old wood paneling which lined each wall had been kept, as well as the small stained glass windows. Although it had been converted into the artist's storage room and refrigerated for the preservation of the paintings, it still spoke of Fannie's presence. I took a deep breath of satisfied pleasure.

"I must go now," firmly stated our guide, ushering us back to the stairwell. "Wait," she called as we were leaving. "Ms. Markwood left something for you." She reached for a sheaf of papers on an entrance hall table.

When we reached the Hotel lobby, I glanced down at the papers. They contained a complete listing of everything printed about the Hotel des Artistes since its beginning in 1917. A goldmine of information, a gift which would save hundreds of research hours, I stared at it incredulously. The image of Fannie's banyan tree appeared superimposed over the words on the page. I was as certain of the gift-giver as of the gift itself.

Carol Ann and I arrived fifteen minutes late for our 7:30 Café reservations the night we'd be meeting Ray Kinstler and the Newmans for the first time. Polly, Annette, and Olga greeted us as we entered, already seated at the front round table just inside the Café door. Susanna Fodor and Ruth appeared moments later. Next came Ray, handsome and smiling warmly. The Newmans followed. Arnold and Gus were gracious and easy to be with from the first introductions.

It proved to be, once again, a magical evening. Stories, memo-

Helen at the Café des Artistes with (left to right), Augusta Newman, Susanna Fodor, Polly Pedjoe, Annette Trembly, Ray Kinstler, Carol Ann Kendrick, Olga Steckler, Arnold Newman.

ries, and questions flowed in dizzying succession. My head spun with joy. Hours flew by.

The Newmans had brought an assortment of prized photographs of the Café taken many years earlier. Faces from the past—those who had lived in the Hotel and those who had been Café devotees—emerged to join us in spirit. The Langs, though not present, sent elegant snifters of brandy.

At two on Sunday afternoon, Carol Ann and I stood outside the apartment owned by Arnold and Gus. Located in the grand old Atelier building on West 67th St., the hotel atmosphere was elegant with age and history. Arnold's powerful photograph of Picasso stood guard beside the doorway.

Beyond the entry area lay a magnificent living room: soaring-ceilinged as befitted an artist's studio. A wall of windows allowed northern light to flood the huge room. One long wall held a number of African artifacts: black ebony figures and ivory carvings interspersed among tribal masks starkly exhibited on a white background. Across the room flashed framed jewels of modern art, each work a masterpiece.

Arnold led us through a back hall, the dining room, and a study. We viewed the Newman collection of Arnold's own work. Hanging in dramatic simplicity, each face told a story: Eugene O'Neill, Ansel Adams, Georgia O'Keeffe, and Grandma Moses. I walked from one to the next in awe.

Over tea and snacks we chatted for a while. Then I asked to see the photograph of Nancy Christy which Arnold had mentioned the previous evening. He rose, nodding for me to follow. There were a half dozen fabulous shots taken in the Christy studio. Nancy posed regally amid the canvases.

The Newmans spoke a bit about their friendship with Picasso. It was an intriguing story and I longed to hear more. "Next time I'll tell you about Stravinsky," Arnold said as we turned to voice a final good-bye.

Ray had invited us to stop by his studio-home around four. The cab pulled to a halt in front of what appeared to be a turn-of-the-century mansion directly facing Gramercy Park. A beautiful ironwork door framed the National Arts Club entrance. We walked into a marbled foyer where a graceful bronze statue stood in a circular stone fountain.

A moment later Ray appeared, descending the staircase steps to greet us. "I'm glad you're here," he said, giving both of us hugs in warm Ray-style. "I've a lot to show you."

The room we entered was elegant. A high stained glass Tiffanyesque ceiling allowed in the afternoon light. Walls and a long bar complemented each other in dark woods polished to satin. Ray went about the room turning on lamps. We were the only people, it seemed, enjoying the place at that hour.

"This was the Samuel Tilden mansion," Ray announced, and in perfect tour guide fashion, continued to relate the history of the place. "Tilden was governor of New York, once even ran for the presidency. At his death, the mansion was deeded to the Arts Club. As you can see, hundreds of American artists are represented here."

Indeed the walls of adjoining rooms were covered in magnificent paintings. It was a visual feast.

"Several movies have been made here," Ray stated. "*Manhattan Murder Mystery* and *The Age of Innocence*."

After exploring the sumptuous first floor area, Ray led us down a long hallway to a rear elevator.

"Now it's time to see my place." We exited several floors upward. Ray walked to a vivid red door. "Here we are."

Ray's living room was charming and comfortable. Paintings bedecked every wall. His powerful, yet understated, technique was obvious in both his portraits and several delightful interior family scenes. Katherine Hepburn, (caftan-swathed and imperial), Liv Ullman, Leonard Bernstein, and many other well-known faces appeared. Equally enthralled, Carol Ann and I moved from one work to the next.

"Come on in here," Ray called from a different room. "This is my studio. I want you to see it while the light is still good." He stood by the windowed wall. The room had a balcony, as had Christy's des Artistes home. A huge easel held a nearly-finished portrait of George Bush. There were numerous canvases stacked about the room, hanging from the walls, and laid amidst piles of photographs, books, correspondence—a cornucopia of a working artist's treasures.

There were stories to be told about each piece, and Ray patiently spoke of "Monty's" guidance as he pointed out Flagg's easel. "This is a special favorite of mine," Ray announced, bringing a framed work from an adjoining hallway. It was Christy's small portrait of Mrs. James Montgomery Flagg.

"Many pieces in my collection have gone to the National Portrait Gallery, my own work and others also. But I can't part with this one." I was pleased to see an example of what Ray termed "Mr. Christy at his finest."

There, too, was a reproduction of Ray's portrait of John Wayne, complete with Stetson, bandana and hands on hips. "That was done for the cover of *The Saturday Evening Post* magazine," Ray explained. "The original is in the Cowboy Hall of Fame in Oklahoma City."

We followed him to the window seat. He had pulled out newspaper and magazine articles, correspondence, auction data, anything relating to Christy he could find. Much of the information was new to me. When we'd finished sifting through the material, the outside light had softened to dusk.

It was time to go. Ray accompanied us back to the lobby. "This has been great for me, too," he said. He hugged us both one more time, ushered us into our taxi, and waved us on our way.

10

I'd been back home from New York for several days when I got a message on my answering machine. "The Christy Quest is booming." Ray sounded excited. "I just got back from Washington, where my Elizabeth Dole portrait was presented. Bob and Elizabeth Dole took me to lunch in the Senate dining room after the ceremony. I looked up and there was Christy's portrait of Sam Rayburn. It was hanging right over our table." I was pleased with that interesting bit of news. But there was more.

"On Monday, right after you left, I met a woman at the National Arts Club named Urania Christy Tarbet." He paused, cleared his throat and continued. "She's a niece of HCC, lives in California, and is a well-known artist herself—pastels. I told her that our Christy group had been in the Café only a few evenings before on Friday night. I gave her your name. She's very eager to talk with you."

I carefully wrote down her name, address, and phone number as Ray spelled them out. The next morning I dialed the number and left as lengthy a message as the Tarbet telephone tape permitted, and waited for a response. It came that same evening.

Urania was as enthusiastic to share her Christy background as I was. We talked for an hour and a half. She told me a wonderful story: When she was a little girl, she was taken to meet her "Uncle Howard" at his studio in the Hotel des Artistes. (Christy was a cousin to Urania's father.) She found Christy charming—warm and smiling. He hugged her immediately and offered her a pen and paper to try out her artistic talent. That was the beginning of Urania's lifelong career. She wholeheartedly credited this meeting as the inspiration which guided her progress as an artist. "Uncle Howard was a beacon of light to me then, and he still is today," she told me. She worked in all media, but primarily pastels, and had held workshops throughout the world.

As we talked on, she spoke of her life with her husband, Bob, and their family, and of a deep affection for their ranch in California. "Please come visit us here," she said. "Come soon." I knew that I would.

"One more thing," she added as we were voicing our good-byes. "I spoke with a woman in Houston who dresses as a Christy Girl and gives lectures on the artist. Her name is Darlene McNaughton."

Soon afterward I punched in Darlene's number. We, too, talked for an hour or so, sharing the mutual delight of our interest in Christy. Almost as an afterthought as we were saying good-bye, Darlene said, "I almost forgot to mention my friend Dorothy Thomas, who also lives in Houston. She modeled for Christy. You must get in touch with her."

The name touched an immediate response in me. I'd had a close friendship with Betty Thomas, whose real name was Dorothy Elizabeth. Betty had died several months earlier. I'd been with her during doctor visits, hospital check-ins and stays, and chemotherapy treatments.

I especially treasured our last visits together. During one of these, she had shared her earnest hope that I would continue the Christy Quest, no matter what. Hearing about my "adventuring" had inspired her. I was moved by her faith and clung to that conversation many times when my spirit sagged.

I was out of state when Betty died. I missed her funeral and burial, physically if not emotionally. I wanted to visit her grave as soon as I returned. I needed some time there as a kind of closure. It helped to stand in the peaceful cemetery setting. I experienced her presence very strongly.

"Betty," I said, "I miss you so much. I miss your wisdom, humor, and faith, and your Christy support. If you can hear me, what would you have me know?"

The wind ruffled leaves, scattering them around my feet. I looked down. My gaze fell on the pink granite marker next to Betty's grave. The single name "Christy" was etched upon the stone. "Thank you, my friend," I whispered and walked back to my car.

Darlene had told me that Dorothy Thomas was elderly, but vivacious and still quite active. Her high-rise apartment was elegant. She had known Christy well and, Darlene stated, "Dorothy insists that she is the redhead on the Café walls."

I was thrilled to hear those words. I whipped out a pen and paper almost before I hung up the telephone and wrote a note to Dorothy, asking if I might call her. I told her of my interest in Christy. I waited a week or so, giving my letter time to arrive. Finally, I could bear it no longer and dialed Dorothy's Houston number. After several rings, I heard a rich, deep-voiced, "Hello."

I introduced myself. Dorothy immediately recognized my name with a warm response. "Of course, Helen. I am so glad you called. I'd love to talk with you about Poppy." She sailed into a fascinating description of her first meeting with the artist.

In the 1930s Dorothy and her mother attended a party in New York which Howard and Nancy Christy attended. Christy approached Dorothy's mother with a bold announcement. "Hello. You have a beautiful daughter. I'd love to paint her." From that moment, a close friendship began which lasted until the deaths of both Christys.

"Poppy painted a fabulous portrait of me soon after our first meeting. I have it. You must come and see it," Dorothy went on almost breathlessly. "And," she continued, "You know I am on the Café des Artistes walls."

I was so excited I could barely respond. "Oh, Dorothy, what a gift this is, finding you."

Dorothy, once into her memories, talked on and on. My hand flew over the yellow pad I always kept by the phone. I couldn't keep up with her. Her life had been fast-paced, exciting. She had lived and traveled the world.

"I married a DuPont, you see," she explained. "I had a home on Majorca. I lived in Peru. I sang and danced on stage and film. My show closed the Rainbow Room, a fabulous finale." Dorothy's voice sang with remembered joy.

"But how—?" I began.

She read my mind at once. "Later I married the love of my life, a Texas oil man, and we moved to Houston. He died some years ago." Dorothy launched into an intriguing history of her friendship with the Christys. "I was so young and so shy when I first met them," she indicated. "And 'Pop' wanted to paint me into the Café murals—nude. I expressed my reticence to pose in that way, and Nancy took my hands in her own. She said, 'Oh, Dorothy, please do this for Howard. The murals will be so beautiful, and I promise you, in perfect taste.'"

She paused for a moment and went on with her story. "Well, I finally agreed. And I became the redhead on those walls. I'm on the cover of George Lang's Café cookbook, too."

And indeed she was. I glanced at my copy of the book as she spoke. How many times had I wondered who she was—the elusive beauty in so many of the tropical settings. Elise Ford (and her sister, Doris, I believed) were easily recognizable. But who was the luscious redhead? The tantalizing mystery had now been solved, but in a far more tangible way than I dreamed possible. Her identity had come forth, vibrantly alive and miraculously in my own home state, a mere few hours away.

"Just before Pop died, Nancy called me," she continued. "He wouldn't go to a doctor. He was a staunch believer in Christian Science. Nancy needed my support in persuading him to get medical help. She said that he closeted himself off in his bedroom with Elise. They read Christian Science literature to each other. He just refused anything else."

Dorothy sighed. "I wasn't at home when Nancy called. I've always regretted that. Nancy was devastated when Pop died. I stayed very close to her during those years. We took her on jaunts up and down the Hudson on Alfred's [DuPont] boat just to get her out of the apartment. She kept it, the apartment, exactly as it had been when Pop lived and painted there."

I had many questions for her, but decided to let her memories unfold as they might.

"You know what?" Dorothy suddenly veered into the present. "I realize as I speak how much my life has held in terms of exciting adventures, money, and all it brought with it: hobnobbing with rich and famed personalities, furs, jewels, on and on. I guess there isn't anything the world offers that I've missed. But, do you know what I am at heart?"

I couldn't imagine what she might say. I knew, however, from the tone in her voice that it was important to her. "No, Dorothy," I replied quickly, "but I'd love to know."

"Well, the truth is," she stated, "I'm just a little girl from Texas. I grew up in a small town right here in the state. I was born in Waco."

I was stunned. "Dorothy! That's really amazing. My family is from Waco. Both my mother and father were born there. It's been like my second home. What a fascinating coincidence. My maiden name was Fason."

It was Dorothy's turn to be stunned. "Helen," she spoke my name with deliberation. "Helen, I grew up going to your granddad Fason's watermelon stand! Every summer, it was one of the treats of my life."

I was too overcome to say a word.

"I know your Aunt Mary. Is she still living? And I took dancing lessons with Florine Fason. Isn't she your aunt also?" Dorothy asked with growing excitement.

I was trying to grasp the odds of such a coincidence. I'd wondered from time to time during the Christy Quest if I might discover a personal connection to the artist. Now I had been given just that. Christy's friend, the Café's mystery model, was not only alive and reachable in my home state, but she had just provided me with an intensely personal link to my own family.

I met Darlene and Paul MacNaughton when they came to Dallas from their Houston home to see the two Christy religious works at the Biblical Arts Center. The following spring Darlene invited Carol Ann and me to her "Christy History" talk before the Houston branch of the Daughters of the Texas Republic. As a certified genealogist, Darlene had researched a Christy-Sam Houston family connection. When she gave her talk, she dressed as a Christy Girl. With her natural blonde beauty and slim figure, she was a lovely embodiment of the artist's ideal of American femininity. After I attended Darlene's presentation, I wanted to visit Dorothy Thomas. I called Celia Lightfoot to join us. Celia was yet another miracle in my life.

Several months earlier, David was having lunch with Weldon Mahan, a close friend from his Dallas office. During their conversation, David mentioned my interest in Christy, including my dream of getting a film funded.

Weldon listened with interest. A slow smile crossed his face, "David, I might be able to help—or my sister might." He explained that Celia Mahan Lightfoot worked with a group called SAM, Southwest Arts Media Productions, which aided prospective filmmakers in getting funds to produce television scripts.

"The office is in Houston," Weldon added. "Why don't you suggest that Helen get in touch with her?" David, surprised, answered, "That just happens to be her next Christy trip."

I called Celia right away. She responded to my proposed idea of a Christy film or documentary with, "Helen, I am so glad you called. What you are describing is exactly what I do. It's my job to a T."

We talked on, discovering personal connections of our own: Celia too was from Waco, knew members of my family, and had gone to college with a mutual friend.

She was enthusiastic and positive about my film vision, promising the board's aid in getting started. We met again later in the month when I visited Houston for a glimpse of two beautiful paintings by Christy in a private downtown club there. The pieces were reminiscent of the Café murals and could have been, I felt, created to hang there. Their history, unfortunately, was lost or unavailable. Two nude figures represented the fall and spring seasons. I assumed they were Elise and Doris.

On the morning of Darlene's talk, Carol Ann and I arrived at the historic log cabin restored by the Daughters of the Texas Republic and now used as their headquarters.

Paul MacNaughton, there to help Darlene set up her Christy display, met us at the door and ushered us in. Darlene looked lovely and calm, unperturbed by the crowd of women milling about, sipping coffee and chatting.

"Dorothy is here!" Darlene announced as we made our way toward her. "She's in the front row. Come, and I'll introduce you." At almost the same moment, I spied Celia as she entered with her video camera. She had offered to film Darlene's talk and afterward Dorothy at her apartment.

A Christy Girl, ca. 1905

Darlene McNaughton
as a Christy Girl, 1994

Dorothy was splendid in silk and pearls. With wit and charisma she charmed everyone who stood in line to meet her. I adored her immediately. She reminded me of Olga, not so much physically, as in attitude. She was exuberant about her life, happy to be who she was, and eager to share her experiences.

"That's me on the cover of the Café book," she reminded us, gesturing toward Darlene's Christy exhibit. Celia's video camera filmed the scene. When Darlene moved toward the lectern to begin her talk, we settled into our seats.

Darlene expertly traced a bit of her own history, weaving it into Christy's career, family origins, and lifestyle. She was a gifted speaker, at ease and fluent behind the podium. Her talk ended far too soon for me. Then we were off to Dorothy's apartment.

Dorothy was waiting for us at the lobby door when Carol Ann and I arrived. As we waited at the elevator, she broke into an impromptu soft-shoe dance, using her black ebony walking cane as a prop. We were delighted.

It was obvious that Dorothy's apartment would be fabulous, judging by the giant double doors which stood at the entry. Feeling a bit like Alice in Wonderland, I peeked inside. I was unprepared for the eclectic and artistic splendor with which it shone.

"Be sure to notice the screen," stated Dorothy. "It belonged to Eva Peron. I once lived in Argentina." We could not have missed it—its huge panels separated the entrance court from the living room beyond. Celia hurriedly unpacked the video camera, eager to capture as much of the setting as possible.

Like ladies-in-waiting, we trailed our queen through room after room as she pointed out furnishings and artifacts. She skillfully blended her personal history with stories of the acquisition of pieces rare and beautiful. Her life unfolded with her steps —and this was certainly a trip she relished. She glowed with the joy inherent in each memory. We were an appreciative audience, spellbound by her flowing accounts of Ascot races, voyages on the "Queen" and the Orient Express, sojourns in Majorca and China, meetings with royalty, and scenes from her career on the stage and screen. She spoke wistfully of her wedding to the Texas oilman and described the elaborate sari which he brought from India for her wedding dress. It was re-designed and stitched by a prominent New York couturier.

Dorothy

As we wandered from room to room, Dorothy spoke into the camera. It would be, I hoped, an intimate commentary on a life truly savored by a lady who pictured the American dream. When we wound our way back to the central living area, we stood before the huge Christy portrait of Dorothy as a young beauty. Two small seascapes by the artist glowed from a side wall, gifts signed "To Dorothy."

"What I wouldn't give," I whispered to Carol Ann, "to take Dorothy back to New York for an evening at the Café des Artistes." She nodded in shared feeling. As Dorothy posed beside her portrait, Celia asked, "How and why did you decide to go to New York from Waco?"

Dorothy smiled a bit wickedly. "The stage, darling, the stage." And she followed her statement with the song and dance routine we'd sampled earlier. Before our eyes Dorothy became the Broadway chorine she had once been. Delighted, we clapped and cheered her on. This experience held a special impact for me. Dorothy's family history and mine had merged a long time ago. Although our lives had taken very different paths, we had been brought together by the artist who inspired us both.

11

Carleen Smith flew with Carol Ann and me to Washington in the summer of 1994. We had exciting prospects: at the forefront, both the Bulkeleys and the Tebbutts had invited us to visit them. We'd be visiting the archives of several institutions, from the National Postal Museum to the Air and Space Museum.

The D.C. weather was beautiful—clear and blue-skied with a fresh breeze—a wonderful welcome from the usual summer mugginess. We picked up our rental car and were off to Arlington National Cemetery.

We played tourist there, watching the always spectacular changing of the guard. It was a perfect beginning. A throng of visitors from all over the world stood in reverent silence as the highly disciplined marines marched in cadence.

We were there to visit the Talbott family gravesite. The cemetery office punched my information into their computer, and the screen printed out the grid map indicating the Talbott plot. We drove up the hillside, following the directions. The Talbott marker was classic and simple.

Ethelyn's face flowed into my mind as I looked at the gray stone. I was glad she had touched my life.

Turning to leave, I looked over at the much larger marble monument beside the Talbott grave. Erected in tribute to those who gave their lives during the Spanish-American War, this marker listed those names. It was another interesting connection: Christy's fame really began with his San Juan battle sketches commissioned in 1898. He'd known Teddy Roosevelt's Rough Riders and watched them in action on Cuban soil. In a few days, we would visit Judge Harry Tebbutt, who owned the artist's original drawing of Colonel Roosevelt.

On a drizzly Friday evening we pulled into the Tebbutt's driveway. Our Washington trip was drawing to a close. It had been, as I'd expected, a fast-paced and exciting adventure. I had found many new friends and a lot of Christy information. We had photocopied a mass of data, searched through files and library stacks, video-taped and shot several rolls of film, walked miles of Capitol, Pentagon, and Smithsonian halls, and viewed dozens of Christy works. Touring the National Air and Space facility in Suitland, Maryland, had been a highlight. We had been allowed to view Christy's great portrait of his friend Captain Eddie Rickenbacker in their "cold vault." When we visited the Naval Art Museum within the Naval Yard, we pored over Christy works with the curator, Gail Monroe. Gail also escorted us on a tour of the Pentagon, where two Christy portraits were exhibited.

At each stop along the way, we were met with enthusiasm and support for the Christy Quest. Carol Ann and I were beginning to pick up research techniques, and Carleen provided a capable third set of hands. The nicest aspect of each appointment was the fun we had. Although hard and intense work (especially sorting through the Juley collection photographs and the voluminous Capitol files), we enjoyed sharing backgrounds with those we met.

Hearing our car, Harry and Jane Tebbutt came outside to welcome us. Theirs was a charming house in a neighborhood of lovely old trees. Feeling at ease with the handsome couple right away, we were launched into a most enjoyable visit. Christy's "Teddy" drawing perfectly captured the bravado of Colonel Roosevelt and, from sword to jaunty stance, the bespectacled figure exhibited the artist's youthful expertise.

The next day we saw the portrait of the dynamic genius who had laid the Atlantic cable, Cyrus Field. This Christy work was housed in the Smithsonian's Arts and Industries Building. After that, we were free to visit the Bulkeleys.

"Come out anytime," the Admiral had said. "We've marked off the week for you." Giving us instructions on how to find their home, Alice ended with, "The Admiral will have the flag flying for you!" Don Quixote or not, I thought, this will be a rare adventure.

True to the Admiral's promise, the Stars and Stripes waved us into the Bulkeley's Silver Springs driveway. We had just parked our car when the Admiral emerged from his front door. Behind him came Alice, petite and almost hidden by her khaki-uniformed husband. I threw down the heavy bag I was carrying and ran up the sidewalk to hug them both. It was a wonderful moment. John Bulkeley fit my mental image of what a retired naval hero would look like: strong and sure, gruff but kind and with an adventurous gleam in his eyes. "H. Alice" was dear, as pretty as a little bird and with a slight British accent which complemented her soft words.

"Come in, mates," announced the Admiral. "These are our quarters." We followed his hefty figure inside and looked about. Every space in the living room was filled with naval memorabilia. The Admiral obviously lived his career.

"Please sit down," said Alice, with a chuckle, "if you can find a spot." We wandered about the room, exploring the artifacts with fascination. The Admiral seemed to relish our interest, explaining what each piece represented. Gradually, he and Alice led us through every room in their home, describing the multifaceted history of their long lives. Offered the opportunity to hold several of the many medals which "Admiral John" (as I began to call him) had received, we placed them in our hands carefully.

"The Admiral has more medals than anyone in the world," Alice proudly told us.

"That is awesome," I said. In my right hand rested the Medal of Honor. Minutes merged into an hour, then another and another. Alice made tea. We took a roll of pictures: the Admiral signing his book, *The Sea Wolf*, for each of us; me holding the Bulkeley ancestral Claymore sword from Scotland; Carol Ann and Carleen gazing at photographs of Admiral John's famed PT Boat.

Alice and Admiral John Bulkeley with Helen

"Come out here," motioned the Admiral, pointing to the back door. We descended the half dozen steel mesh steps leading down to the patio. "You've just walked on history," grinned the Admiral, "I brought those steps from the battleship *Missouri* on which the World War II peace treaty was signed. It was an unforgettable experience."

We were deeply moved by Admiral John's description of the landing on Omaha Beach. He captured into words the chain of events which led to the fiftieth anniversary of D-Day.

"We go back to the Normandy beaches every year," Alice informed us. "But this year, of course, was a huge celebration."

Out came the scrapbook holding their snapshots of all the festivities. "I had to stick right by President Clinton," Admiral John snorted. "The brass figured he'd be less likely to be shot at if a war hero was next to him."

We spoke from time to time of their friendship with Howard and Nancy Christy.

"We four were quite close," said Alice. "We lived only a few blocks from them in New York City after the war. They came to the hospital each time we had a baby and you know, we have four children. Three of them were born there."

Christy had given the Bulkeleys a small oil painting, a beach scene. "Howard always said that we were a romantic couple. He pictured us at the seaside," Alice explained and smiled shyly. She had been a young girl in China when Admiral John's ship was anchored there. "Actually, my husband rescued me," she continued. "Bombs were exploding everywhere. Even our home was burned. My husband brought me on board his ship. It was a dreadful time." Her eyes misted as she spoke of the war camp her family was sent to. "My father died there. I never saw him again."

Each question we asked brought forth memories for the couple. They both enjoyed sharing what had been a most eventful life together. Abruptly, it seemed, it had become late afternoon.

"Can't you stay for dinner?" Alice queried "We can go out, or I'll fix something here.

"Please do," the Admiral seconded his wife. "We've only gotten started, you know. You haven't seen the basement yet."

We asked for a raincheck, knowing we should be on our way, but touched by their warm invitation.

"You'll keep us posted on the Christy Quest?" Alice called from the front porch as we climbed into the car. It had been hard to leave. Every time we headed for the door, one or the other of us spied an object, picture or book to ask about. At last, regretfully, we had one last farewell hug and climbed into the car. As we pulled away, I looked back. The American flag moved gently above the Bulkeleys who stood together, arms entwined.

12

I decided to surprise Carol Ann with a trip to the Kentucky Derby for her birthday in 1996. We planned to drive from Dallas, taking several weeks to antique and Christy-research along the way. I wanted to start with the Truman Library at Independence, Missouri, where Christy's portrait of Alben Barkley hung on a wall leading into the replica of the Truman Oval Office.

It proved to be a fruitful stop, for the curator gave us new material. I'd forgotten that Barkley was a native Kentuckian, a bit of knowledge that underlined our journey. And I didn't realize the high regard which the vice-president and Christy held for each other. Christy had been present in Independence for the unveiling of his Barkley portrait.

Our next Christy stop was at Stephens College in Columbia, Missouri, where Christy's pastel portrait of the actress Maude Adams is displayed. It was a joy to view young Maude, posed as "Babbie" during her Broadway performance in J. M. Barrie's *The Little Minister*. Her long career had been stellar—both in technique and in popularity. On her retirement, she had been persuaded by the Stephens faculty to join their drama department. She remained at the college for thirteen years, continuing to inspire students. After her death, an award in her name was instituted by an alumnae group. It had been presented four times since its inception.

A magnificent cameo inspired by Christy's portrait of Maude

was designed in Italy for each recipient. Previous awards had gone to Helen Hayes, Agnes Moorhead, and Julie Harris. The fourth presentation of the Maude Adams award had taken place on the weekend before Carol Ann and I arrived. It was given to Lynn Redgrave, who had been in Columbia for the ceremony.

Carol Ann and I antiqued to our heart's delight as we drove toward Kentucky. Our car was already packed with various treasures, bits and pieces of yesteryear. An antique-finders guide told us of a strip of small villages called Antique Alley off the main highway. As we sped along the interstate, I was navigating, map in hand. I had marked the cutoff to the Indiana countryside. A few minutes later, a thought popped into my mind. I opened the map again.

"Why don't we cut across the state now? We have time, and we might run into something interesting in these little towns before we get to the antique trail."

We did so and were greeted with several picturesque villages along the countryside. I liked the rural quiet of Indiana. The farms were neat, as were the main streets of small towns. We drove into Greenfield, a county seat boasting a wonderful courthouse and central square.

"I'm hungry," I announced. "Let's stop here for lunch." Carol Ann agreed, and we circled the square on the lookout for a cafe. As we did so, we spied a large bronze statue posted on the courthouse lawn.

"Stop!" I called out, not knowing why I felt such urgency. Carol Ann braked quickly, a bit irritated at my sharp command. "Pull over so we can read the name on the statue," I ordered. The name imprinted on the bronze was James Whitcomb Riley.

"This must be Riley's hometown! We've got to find out."

"Well, we won't have to go far to do that," she answered, "There's a sign over there that says 'J. W. Riley's Home and Museum in the next block."

Hunger forgotten, I couldn't wait to get to the two sites. The many Riley books which Christy had illustrated swam in my mind. His drawings were simple and charming, ideally enhancing Riley's poetic stories. I'd found copies of *An Old Sweetheart of Mine, Out to Old Aunt Mary's, When She Was Sweet Sixteen, Riley's Roses,* and had grown to love them all. As a child, I'd read, re-read and memorized *Orphan Annie,* caught by the cadence of the poem and its wonderful story. Riley had, in fact, inspired the "Little Orphan Annie" comic strip and the Raggedy Ann doll.

"Here we are," stated Carol Ann, pulling up in front of a clapboard house. I was out of the car before the ignition was off and bounding up the front porch steps of Riley's home.

Several Greenfield ladies greeted me as I entered. I took a quick tour and then walked next door to the Riley Museum. I'd find his books and papers there, they told me. The museum door was opened by a tiny elderly woman who might have been Riley's "Aunt Mary." She ushered me in, explaining as we stood in the front hall that she was a bit "hard of hearing and had trouble speaking."

I understood her perfectly, however, and was touched by her sweetness. She seemed so happy that I had come. I told her why I was excited to be in Riley's hometown and of the Christy connection in my life.

"If only my husband were here," she offered. "He could tell you about Riley better than I. He should be back soon." I decided to ask Carol Ann about a possible return after lunch. She was waiting in the car, nursing a headache. I could see a fine looking elderly gentleman at the curb.

"Hello" he approached and offered his hand. "How was your tour of the museum?" I replied that it had been wonderful, and I pulled out my Christy business card.

"I'm writing my own story about Howard Chandler Christy," I explained. He stared at the card and then at me.

"This is really something," he said. "How did you know to come here?"

"I didn't." I laughed. "I just came on an impulse. I had no idea about Riley or Greenfield."

He shook his head slightly, "Well, do you know that you are our first visitor? Today is the first day the museum has been open, and we opened at noon."

My watch read 12:20. I must have knocked at noon, a few minutes more or less. I was stunned by the timing.

He introduced himself as Edward Eggleston and told me he was the great-nephew of the famed Indiana author of the same name. He talked on in his own excitement. "For you to be our first visitor—this is wonderful. My wife and I will be in touch with you later. We'll do some Christy research here. It will give us a project, and we've needed one. I can't wait to tell her."

I glanced toward the car. Carol Ann's head rested on the steering wheel. I realized that we needed lunch and bade good-bye to Mr. Eggleston. After some food and a couple of aspirins, Carol Ann began to feel better.

We were antique browsing in a shop on Main Street when I heard my name called. From the mall's second floor landing I gazed down into the upturned face of Mr. Eggleston.

"Can you come back to the museum?" he called up breathlessly. "My wife has something to show you." His face glowed with pleasure. Our car followed his back down the street to the small museum. Mrs. Eggleston waited at the open front door, beaming with anticipation as she led us into the library.

"I found all the books illustrated by Christy," she said and proudly gestured toward a table in the center of the room. Each copy, signed by Riley's "J.W.R.", was opened and lovingly laid out for my inspection. I was familiar with each one, but I didn't tell her so. The joy of her discovery and the delight in her gift tugged at my heart.

"You've given us such pleasure," Mr. Eggleston said. "Your visit lets us know that the museum *is* important."

I couldn't express the happiness I felt in being drawn to this place—nor, I suppose, could they. The Greenfield experience was an example of what I loved most about the Christy Quest —bringing together people who might not otherwise meet. And somehow in the process of joining, the energy produced fueled my adventure and encouraged others as well.

As we drove past the courthouse, I saluted Indiana's Hoosier Poet. I was glowing with gratitude.

"You look like you just swallowed the canary," Carol Ann said.

I grinned back in return, and settled into the car seat with satisfaction.

Carol Ann and I joined the city's excitement when we arrived in Louisville on the evening before Derby Day. Banners and flags were flying everywhere. Streams of traffic merged onto the highways. Buses, vans, and limousines from all over America were converging on this spot. In the crowded lobby of our Holiday Inn mint juleps flowed. Red roses graced ticket booths and banquet tables. We checked in, unpacked our silk dresses and picture hats, and rang for room service.

Our bus was scheduled to leave the motel at nine Saturday morning. We were hatted and dressed with time left to watch the lobby parade for half an hour. Eccentric outfits were the rule. Some were outlandishly ornamented with sequins and glitter, feathers and fur. Headgear created to equal Hedda Hopper's best chapeaus swayed back and forth on freshly coifed hairdos. Rain was predicted and the sky was covered in gray low-lying clouds, but no one seemed to mind.

We were both unprepared for the mass of people already milling about at Churchill Downs when we arrived. We walked for what seemed miles before we left the parking lot. The grandstand above the huge oval track loomed in the distance like a mirage. Finally, we reached the entrance gates and took our place in line. Once inside, ticket stubs in hand, we looked about in bewilderment. It would be, we realized, a major accomplishment to weave through the packed crowd. A long hour later we found our seats, sat down in relief, and kicked off our shoes. Once settled, we could relax and take in the spectacle itself.

The Run for the Roses was to take place around 5 P.M. The preceding races, colorful crowd, and magnificent horses all added to the increasing anticipation. Finally, here it was—a kaleidoscope of sound and color which crescendoed into the heart-stopping three minutes for which we had come. Red-coated musicians marched onto the field. The horses danced nervously in their gate positions. Some 148,000 Derby fans stood in an awed silence as the first bars of "My Old Kentucky Home" pealed across the air. As if on cue—and it could have been no other way—the sun broke through the cloud cover, gracing all below with shafts of light. It all came together in a rush of emotion, and I cried with the joy of the experience. The last of Stephen Foster's immortal words died away, the trumpets sounded, and they-were-off!

Sunday, still exhilarated by the pageant, we lazed about our room, breakfasted in bed, and watched every scrap of Derby news on TV. On Monday we picked up the Christy Quest again. Christy had painted one of Kentucky's favorite governors, A. B. {Happy) Chandler. The two men had a lot in common. Both were known for their boisterous, jovial nature. The Chandler name belonged to both. Although no genealogical link had been forged between the two, each enjoyed referring to the other as "cousin."

Happy's grandson was the current attorney general of Kentucky. It was as good a place as any to start, so I called Ben Chandler's office in Frankfort, Kentucky's capital. He was away, but through that office I found Happy's son, also Ben, who was the editor of the newspaper in Versailles. The Chandlers were in the middle of moving into the Chandler home place, but I reached Mrs. Chandler—Toss. She was warm and interested in the Christy project. We were invited to view the portraits of Governor and Mrs. Chandler which hung in the family home.

Versailles lies in the heart of Kentucky's beautiful horse country. We drove unhurriedly through the green fields, spiked with white picket fences. The town itself was charming—clean and neat and rather old-fashioned. We found a tearoom and settled in for a delicious lunch. By the time we had finished with the last bite of homemade pie, it was time to find the Chandler home.

Toss met us with a warm hello, apologizing for the stacked cartons lining the long entrance hall. It was a wonderful old house with high-ceilings, Oriental carpets, and mahogany furniture.

As she led us down the hall, she rubbed her back and grimaced in pain. "Forgive me," she explained, "I pulled a muscle last evening lifting a grandchild the wrong way. Sorry."

It was clear that she was in pain, but she gamely smiled and motioned us into the dining room. Christy's portrait of Mildred Chandler hung on the central wall.

"We feel that it is well done, except the dimensions are off. The chair isn't in perspective at all." She was right. Christy's error was obvious at first inspection.

"That's strange," I wondered aloud. "But I guess we'll never know why he left it like that." Although Elise had written of Christy's friendship with the Chandlers, there was nothing specifically about the two portraits.

"Come and see Happy's portrait," said Toss. "It's across in

the living room." Governor Chandler surveyed the comfortable book-lined room from a prominent position above the fireplace. It was, I felt, a fine example of the artist's work.

We sat down with Toss under Happy's visage and chatted for awhile. She was a delightful hostess despite her discomfort. A stunning redhead, she was as witty and bright as she was lovely.

We had planned to meet Don Welch at his store in Shelbyville on our last day in the Bluegrass State. Don had come into my life via Byron Crawford, a writer for the *Louisville Courier* who had left a message on my recorder a year earlier.

When I returned the call, Byron sketched out the fascinating tale of a discovery by a fellow Kentuckian, Don Welch, who owned and operated several warehouses in and around Louisville. He sold, among various other assorted goods, cigarettes. He had bought an old building across from a train depot in a village called Eminence. In clearing out the building, Don carted away truckloads of trash. Ready to dump one final load, something caught his eye. It was a large brightly colored picture. On closer inspection, it proved to be an old Lucky Strike ad. Don pulled it out, shook it off, and was shocked to see that it was an oil painting on canvas.

He decided to do a bit of research. After making several phone calls, he reached the American Tobacco Co. He learned that they had commissioned the painting by Christy in 1939. It had been distributed as a poster throughout the country. No one had any idea how the original oil had found its way to a wall in a building in Eminence.

Amazingly, the work was in perfect condition. Don's growing interest in the painting was fed further when he discovered that it had been affixed to the wall face inward and overlaid with wallpaper. It had been hidden and/or protected on purpose.

Although I didn't know what the painting was worth, I was able to give Byron some background on Christy. He promised to send me a copy of the Lucky Strike article. We agreed to stay in touch. I replaced the phone and thought over the conversation.

The Christy adventure had been sprinkled with "lost" or mystery paintings, from *The Christ* to the missing nudes from the walls of the Café des Artistes and now the intriguing Lucky Strike canvas.

Don was eager, and so were we, to share Christy information. I wanted to see the original Lucky Strike painting. We reloaded our suitcases into an already overpacked car and headed for the highway. We found Don's store with ease. I stopped outside the large front window for a moment, noticing with amusement what had to be the huge painting itself. It had been covered with a drop cloth top to bottom. Don was behind the cash register, busy with a line of customers, but he signaled to us with a grin. I got out my camera and notepad and waited.

"Let's have the unveiling!" Don announced at the first break in the line. "You go outside, and I'll remove the cover."

We did so obediently. Don carefully drew back the heavy spread, then joined us to view his prize displayed in the window. Christy's couple was posed against a brilliant yellow background. The words, "Forever and Ever" hung in the air as did the symbolic circle of smoke between the man and woman. They leaned toward each other, caught in the romance of a marriage proposal. The advertisement was simple, amusing, and eye-catching.

"It's in excellent condition," I said to Don, "as if it had been painted yesterday."

He glowed with pleasure. "I still can't believe it. The way it turned up."

"What are the chances of going to Eminence?" I asked him, "Can you take some time off and drive over with us?"

He nodded in affirmation. "You bet. I want to show you the space on the wall where it was. Then *you* won't believe it!"

The huge painting was carefully rewrapped. Don instructed his stand-in behind the cash register, "I'll be back in an hour," and we headed for his van.

It is a beautiful back-road drive through farm country to the tiny village of Eminence. I loved Don's exuberance and wholehearted support of my Christy research. He had also garnered a great deal of information on the artist.

When we reached Eminence, he pulled to a stop on the picturesque main street and pointed to the building across the way. "That's it there," he boasted, "Isn't it great? It's a landmark.

"Someone, maybe a tobacco salesman, must have brought the painting from the train into the store with him, although why he

Don Welch and his prize

left it here is a mystery."

We walked inside Don's store. He went immediately to the spot where it was found. "It was here," he told us, indicating the wall behind the cash register.

"Why would someone have hidden it there—faced inward and covered with paper?" Carol Ann asked. Each of us offered possible scenarios, letting our imaginations run.

"Whether I ever find the answers or not, I don't really care," Don stated. "It's brought me so much pleasure it doesn't matter."

I understood how he felt. I could no longer imagine my life without "the quest." As we drove out of Eminence toward Shelbyville, I ticked off a mental gratitude list. It just kept getting better.

I had called Byron Crawford the minute we arrived in Louisville, leaving a message on his office phone. He called back later indicating a packed Derby weekend. Our best chance of getting together was for lunch on our way out of Shelbyville. We planned to rendezvous at a restaurant between Shelbyville and Louisville around one. It would be chancy at best, for Byron had scheduled appointments that morning and we were coming from different directions. We made several wrong turns before we found Applebee's, and arrived fifteen minutes late.

"He was here," the waitress informed us, "but he had to leave." Disappointment welled up.

Carol Ann sighed. "We have to eat anyway. Let's sit down and order."

We'd missed Byron by such a close margin, but there was nothing to do but read the menu. We ordered lunch, and I moped.

"Maybe he'll come back," said Carol Ann. I didn't think so, but hope dies hard. I kept looking out our window at the arriving cars. And then it happened. A van drove in and parked. Byron hopped out and headed for the entrance. I recognized him immediately from the newspaper picture beside his column. I leaped up to greet him.

"My schedule is crazy," he grinned. "I didn't think you'd still be here, but I decided to come back anyway."

We had a delightful visit, sharing Christy stories, our own histories and the joy of the Derby. Byron was great—funny, warm, and highly intelligent. Born and bred in Kentucky, he was an ideal representative of the Bluegrass State.

"You'll have to come back, you know," Byron stated as the waitress brought our check, "I think I'll put you both up for membership in the Order of Kentucky Colonels."

Carol Ann and I stared at him. The Colonels had funded the beautiful Christy painting at My Old Kentucky Home State Park in Bardstown. I had talked with their registrar, Mildred Reger, in Louisville before we left Dallas. She had sent material regarding the unveiling ceremony. Both Howard and Nancy Christy were given honorary memberships in the historic order. Chuckling at our appreciation, Byron promised to check on it and let us know.

Now it was time to turn toward home. The sun shone bright on this day, too. Catching one last view of the Louisville skyline, I could swear I heard the Derby bugles.

13

I wanted to explore Christy's California connections. In 1939 he had spent months in Los Angeles painting portraits. His huge United Nations commemorative mural was in San Francisco.

Carol Ann and I flew to California in early September 1996. En route, I pulled out the Smithsonian listings. Six portraits had surfaced in the Los Angeles area: Gene Autry's 1945 portrait at the Museum of Western History; the portraits of Will and Betty Rogers at the Rogers' ranch in Pacific Palisades; portraits of Mr. and Mrs. Edward Doheny at St. John's Seminary in Camarillo; and a fabulous portrait of screen star Norma Talmadge at the Museum of Hollywood History. The seventh portrait, that of Herbert Hoover, was stored in the Hoover Institute at Stanford University. We would fly home from San Francisco after visiting the Herbst Memorial Theatre which housed Christy's United Nations mural.

We landed in Los Angeles on a glorious Saturday afternoon, cloudless and crisp. We had no scheduled appointments until Monday morning, so we could play tourist until then. After lunch at the Farmer's Market, we spied an antique mall across the way and headed for it. The space just next to the mall was occupied by a Christian Science Reading Room. It seemed an odd site, and on impulse I pushed open the door. Carol Ann, surprised, followed.

"I wonder if you could give me information on a portrait of Mary Baker Eddy?" I asked the woman behind a front desk. "It was painted by Howard Chandler Christy."

She didn't know of such a portrait, but she gave us several books to scan. Then her face brightened with an idea. "I do remember something. I was cleaning out some drawers last week and I found a picture I hadn't ever seen before." She bent down to open a drawer underneath the counter. We waited while she rummaged through stacks of papers.

"Here!" She beamed. "I found it."

It was a lovely portrait of Mrs. Eddy, in excellent condition printed on fine quality paper. The color was especially beautiful—muted, yet intense. Best of all, the artist's signature spelled out Christy. I was thrilled to find it, for the founder of Christian Science had made a powerful impact on Christy's life. Information about the portrait's whereabouts had eluded me until this moment. Now I would contact the Mother Church in Boston.

"Here we go again," said Carol Ann as we left the reading room. "Another one of those right-out-of-the-blue deals."

I agreed. "The unexpected gifts may be the best of all."

A month or so before our trip, a friend suggested that I call the Hollywood Chamber of Commerce to see if I could find someone versed in Hollywood art history. Hoping to discover the whereabouts of Christy's portraits of Norma and Constance Talmadge, I did. I was given the name and number of Marc Wanamaker, a well-recognized Hollywood historian.

After I told Marc of my Christy research and upcoming trip to L.A. he said, "You've come to the right place. I can tell you exactly where the portrait of Norma is."

Pen poised, I waited, tingling with the thrill of the chase.

"There is a fabulous museum here," Marc went on. "Not too many people know of it. It's called the Hollywood Studio Museum, but it's really the original Cecil B. DeMille studio, where the first films were made. It has some priceless movie artifacts: Valentino's cape, the chariot from Ben Hur, and the Christy portrait of Norma Talmadge."

The tingling sensation intensified as he continued, "Christy is one of my favorite artists. I have a file on him and I'll send it to you before you leave. Call me when you get here. I'll arrange to meet with you, and we can view it together."

True to his word, his packet arrived within the week. I dug into it. There were a number of photos of Christy posed with Hollywood legends (Will Hayes, William Randolph Hearst, Sid Grauman) and shots taken on movie sets. Nancy appeared in several pictures as well.

The Talmadge sisters, Norma and Constance, were silver screen legends. Norma, a good friend of Sid Grauman, had accidentally stepped into the wet concrete outside his lavish new Chinese Theatre while visiting him there. From that misstep came the idea of preserving the hand and footprints of movie stars.

Grauman's sidewalk thus became the Walk of Stars and one of the most popular tourist attractions in Hollywood. Marc sent photocopies of the interior of the theater in its heyday. Two giant canvases hung in the foyer—Christy's portraits of the Talmadge sisters. I supposed that when Grauman's Theatre was sold, Norma's portrait went to the Hollywood Studio Museum. Constance was still missing.

An expert on movie and art history, Marc was a much sought-after figure. I knew he'd have to juggle his schedule and sandwich us in. He seemed as anxious as I to view the Norma Talmadge portrait, but a snag developed. "The Studio Museum is closed for renovation." My heart fell with the words.

"I'm not about to give up," Marc continued. "I'm on the board there and can get us in, but we have to be accompanied by a museum curator. Several of them are out of pocket, but I'll keep trying." The merry-go-round began. On Sunday, there was hope, on Monday a visit seemed doubtful. On Tuesday morning, the prospects had darkened. We had only one day left before we were to leave early Thursday morning. With every finger crossed, I dialed Marc's number Tuesday evening.

"We're on!" he announced at once. "A curator will meet us at the museum tomorrow afternoon at four. She will have to leave for a meeting across town, but she promised to be there."

I was out of bed before seven on Wednesday morning and turned on the TV to check out the weather. Carol Ann was still asleep so I kept the volume low. A dramatic scene came to life on the screen. A newsman stood outside a burning building. Yellow-slickered firemen moved in the background. The cameraman scanned from right to left, pausing at a sign outside the front of the building. I read the big black lettering, "Hollywood Studio Museum." The words didn't register for a moment, then crashed through.

"Carol Ann!" I wailed. "Get up. The museum is on fire!" Carol Ann sat up slowly and tried to focus. I turned up the sound. We sat in stunned silence, trying to take it in. A homeless indigent had started a fire at the back of the museum which quickly spread through the frame building. It was hoped that some of the equipment and artifacts could be saved. In the hour that followed, we turned from channel to channel. Most stations carried the news of the fire.

"This is unbelievable," I said. "Our meant-to-be turned into a can't-possibly-be. How can it happen on the one day we were going there?" The phone rang.

"Do you have the TV on?" asked Marc. Miserable, I answered that we did, indeed.

"Well, then you know the bad news, but, there's good news, too. Christy's portrait of Norma has been saved. And—we're going in anyway."

"How!?"

Marc explained that the curator had been there since early morning. She would let us inside at four as planned. "I'm more anxious than ever for you to view the portrait," he said. "You can help us appraise it for repair. I'll be in the parking lot watching for you."

I replaced the phone and turned to Carol Ann. "It's not that we're not to see the painting, it's that we're not *not* to see it! Even a fire isn't keeping us out."

When we arrived at the museum, wide yellow tape was strung around the parking lot. Guards strode about. My heart sank. "Please, can we get through?" I asked the guard who halted our car. "We have an appointment with the museum curator." He rubbed his chin with indecision.

"Look, I'll bet that's Marc over there," said Carol Ann. "He's waving to us." The guard looked toward Marc, shrugged, and removed the tape.

Marc trotted over as we parked. He was talking before I got the window down. "Helen, I'm glad you're here, but we've got a problem." I swallowed, dreading to hear what he might say. "The curator is leaving right now. She says she can't wait."

I was out of the car in a flash. "But we're here."

A woman in a yellow running suit came toward us. She thrust out a hand in greeting. "Hi, I'm Hanna. I'm a curator for the museum. I've been here since early morning, and I'm exhausted. I'm so sorry." Hanna was obviously worn out and disheveled.

I tried anyway. "Hanna, please, we'll race in and out. I just want to see the painting. I promise we'll be fast."

Marc was nodding in sympathy. "Please, Hanna, they've come all the way from Texas."

She relented with a tired wave of her hand. "All right. But hurry." She started for the entrance. We were right behind her. Stepping up onto the porch, she suddenly stopped short. We banged together like dominoes.

"Oh, I forgot—it's dark in there, in the side room where the portrait is. You can't see a thing." Plunged into despair again, I scarcely nodded when a man approached and introduced himself as one of the museum staff. He had been, he told us, instrumental in moving the DeMille "barn" to its current site.

"Did I hear you say you needed a flashlight?" he asked. "I have a big one in my car." I could have hugged him on the spot. Hearing our chorus of "Yes!" he wheeled and made for his car. In a moment he was back, armed with a large light.

"You are an angel," I called back to him as we strode single file into the building. Carol Ann and I realized at the same time that we were sloshing through water. Our sandals and feet were soaked.

"Be careful of the wiring," Hanna warned and snaked us through plastic-covered-equipment and artifacts. Everything was jumbled about; it was eerie in the dim light.

"We're going in here," Hanna announced. Marc snapped on the flashlight. Once inside the room, he focused the light on Christy's giant canvas. The face of Norma Talmadge appeared, beautiful and serenely unaware of the destruction about her. The portrait was so large that we could see only small portions at a time. This was certainly the most dramatic viewing of any Christy work so far, standing in water in a pitch-dark room inside a fire-ravaged building. It reminded me of the ballroom scene years before in the Hotel des Artistes with Emma when we had held up matches to see.

Hanna brought me back to the present with her words, "We must go now." We slowly waded back to the entrance and emerged into the sunlight.

Marc offered a visit to his office across from the first Paramount Studios. His car led us through L.A. streets. Once there, Marc hopped from his car and motioned us to follow. He gave us a quick but fascinating walk through the reception area of the original studio.

A few paces later, we were in Marc's small office. It was packed with books, magazines, and papers. He listened to his long list of messages, and then told us a bit about his own background. Educated in art history and furniture design, he had found the Hollywood movie industry a perfect vehicle for his talents. He researched endlessly, traveling about the world as an advisor to film makers. He had curated the DeMille art collection. In response to our question, he stated he was, yes, a nephew of actor and director Sam Wanamaker. He was also in demand as a writer, contributing to many publications, such as *Architectural Digest.*

He had become a decorator of note, aiding many patrons who desired rare objets d'art. The air was charged with his energy and enthusiasm. With his brush of curly hair, huge grey-green eyes and infectious grin, he reminded me of Gene Wilder.

Carol Ann and I viewed the Doheny portraits in Camarillo accompanied by my cousin, Jerry Black. Jerry and her husband, John, lived only a few minutes away from St. John's Seminary. I hadn't seen her in many years, so I was especially grateful for our visit.

St. John's Seminary was lushly gardened with swaying palms and brilliant flowers. The portraits were in the main reading room of the library. It was a beautiful building, and the elevator itself a work of art. The portraits of the handsome couple who had funded the seminary, as well as a great deal of Los Angeles real estate, hung on either side of a fireplace in the huge central room. We felt each was exceptionally painted—Christy's work at its best.

On Monday morning, blessed by beautiful weather and a good

breakfast, we sped down the boulevard leading to Pacific Palisades. We drove past sumptuous Hollywood estates shrouded in palm trees and oleanders. We were headed for the retreat where the Rogers family had lived. It was now a California State Park.

We began the long drive up the mountain, relishing the scenic beauty. From Dallas I talked with Nancy Mendez, the curator of the estate. She promised us a personal tour of the premises. She also suggested we meet with Emil Sandmeier, now ninety-six, who had been Will Rogers' right-hand man on the ranch.

We rounded the last bend, and a park ranger signaled us into the parking area. We stepped from the car, seemingly the sole visitors. The ranger called, "Nancy!" and soon a brisk figure walked toward us. Her brown eyes danced. "I'm so glad you're here. One of our rangers has gone to pick up Emil at his home. They'll be here in a few minutes." I hugged her in gratitude.

"Let's go up to the house. I'll begin the tour there," she said. We trailed after her, up winding steps which led to the wide veranda at the front of the ranch home. The view from the porch was spectacular. A green polo field lay before us, edged and surrounded by the forest itself.

"This is a dream setting." I said, trying to express the tranquillity of the place.

"We've kept it exactly as it was when the family lived here," Nancy told us, as we followed her inside. Years earlier I'd come across a magazine article about the ranch with color layouts of the interior. I knew that one entered a huge central living area furnished in Southwestern style. The dining room formed an adjunct to the sitting room, and the portraits were hanging there. Stepping inside, I felt lifted back in time, as though the close-knit, laughing Rogers clan might appear at any moment. The high ceiling was timbered in old beams. Open harnesses made into lamps hung before the great stone fireplace. Indian woven rugs provided color. A leather calf stood to one side.

"Mr. Rogers was always asked to show off his roping skill," Nancy told us. "A friend gave him the calf as an indoor target."

Sunshine poured in from large plate glass windows at each end of the room. Paintings and sculptures enhanced the scene, works of Russell and Remington among them. The Christy portraits hung on their wide wall.

The front door opened. "Careful, Emil," cautioned the handsome young ranger by an elderly gentleman's side. A comfortable chair was found for Emil, and after settling him into it we were introduced. Born in Switzerland, his accent had remained. He immediately launched into memories of his friend and employer, Mr. Rogers.

An hour or more sped by while we listened raptly to his accounts of life on the ranch. Emil knew every inch of the place, giving us a detailed history of the furnishings. "I lived right up there," Emil stated proudly, "before Mr. Rogers helped me to buy a house." A second, balconied level could be seen above the main floor.

"I lost everything in the Depression," Emil continued. "I had a brand new wife, and I needed a job. Mrs. Rogers put a help-wanted ad in the newspaper. I saw it and was invited out to talk it over. Mrs. Rogers interviewed me. She said she'd let me know after she spoke with Mr. Rogers. Just as I was leaving, she asked me if I could speak French. I was pleased to say that I could. I thought it was a funny question, but she smiled and said, 'That's good.'" Emil paused, rubbed his chin, and grinned, "Well, I got the job. And I guess maybe it was because Mary, their teenage daughter, wanted to study French."

Emil Sandmeier

One reminiscence led to another. "One of my best memories is about the Lindberghs. You know, they were close friends of Mr. and Mrs. Rogers. The Rogers had lost a baby son to an illness. They fell in love with the Lindbergh's baby—he reminded them of their little boy. When the boy was kidnapped, they were heartsick for their friends. They invited the Lindberghs to stay with them during the trial. They accepted, needing a break from the terrible stress in the courtroom. This was a good place to come because the newsmen couldn't get up here. Reporters congregated around the foot of the mountain, down by the gate, just waiting for a glimpse of the Lindberghs. When it came time for them to go back home, we talked about the best way to get them out without the newsmen knowing it."

Emil paused, remembering, and we watched a sly smile cross his face. "It was my idea they used. I suggested taking them out the back way. I had an old car, and we put them in it. It was the middle of the night when we left. We went right through there." He pointed toward the kitchen and continued, "By that time, I had a house of my own. It was close by, so we drove there. We had just moved in. We didn't have much furniture but we did the best we could. The Lindberghs were wonderful guests. They didn't mind a bit. My wife cooked breakfast for them the next morning. We didn't have a dining room table, but we set up a folding card table, and we ate off of it. The reporters never knew a thing."

Emil grinned broadly. "Several weeks later, a great big crate was delivered to us. It was a set of dining room furniture from the Lindberghs. We've kept it all these years. Still use it."

Emil talked about other famous visitors to the ranch—senators, governors, mayors, movie stars, and the Ziegfeld family, who settled nearby.

At last, it was time to leave. We moved out to the veranda and sat with Emil for a few last minutes. "This is the first time I've been here in awhile," he told us. "I've been under the weather. I had surgery." He looked out toward the green field beyond. "It's so good to be back. This will always be home to me."

On Friday we had a three o'clock appointment with Elena Danielson at the Hoover Institute at Stanford, so we kept a steady pace until we reached Palo Alto. We found the Stanford campus teeming with students and parents—it was Freshman Orientation Week.

Elena took us to the archive storage area. The large portrait had already been pulled for viewing. It was a fine portrait of former President Hoover, painted in New York while he was in residence at The Waldorf Towers.

"I think his eyes are sad," Elena commented as we stood before the portrait. "His wife had died recently, and he was lost without her."

Although our visit at the Hoover Institute was brief, I felt it was important. Christy had admired President Hoover, and the portrait commission had pleased him deeply.

We left the sprawling Stanford campus anxious to find a motel. Most were already filled as we'd expected, but at last we found a room. We grabbed it, unloading our bags gratefully. Then I called Mrs. Gladys Woodhams, who also lived in Palo Alto. I'd found her name listed on a printout from the National Portrait Gallery. She owned *Monks In a Great Hall*, a Christy illustration done in gouache.

Luckily, she and her husband were home for the evening and invited us over. Their home was beautiful and graciously furnished. Gladys had collected fine works of art during her lifetime, mostly by American women painters. I loved seeing her Christy piece. It was a perfect example of his early work as a book illustrator.

Our last stop on the California journey was in San Francisco. We rose early to meet with Greg Ridenour, curator-historian at the Herbst Memorial Theatre. Christy's huge mural had an interesting history. It originally hung in the United Nations building in New York. Because it had been executed by an American artist, portraying only the Americans who signed the treaty, various foreign representatives frowned upon it. Under such protest, it had been moved to the Carnegie Endowment Building in New York. Later it found its permanent home in San Francisco. The location made sense, for now it resided on the site where the treaty was actually signed.

The theatre is in the San Francisco Civic Center complex. We peeked inside the heavy doors. An Oriental dance company was rehearsing. Spotlights played over the room as technicians scampered up and down the aisles.

After a few minutes, Greg appeared to lead us into a large adjoining room. "Here is our Christy mural," he said proudly. The huge painting hung high above us. Standing on a tall stool, I was able to see it better.

"I've brought information on the signing of the charter for you," Greg offered. "The ceremony took place right inside the theatre. The upholstered seats were removed, and folding chairs and tables were brought in." Greg had photographs of the event. Christy had captured another momentous event in American history.

The sun shone radiantly as we left the theater and headed for our car. The trip had gone even better than expected. Once again, I realized the power of taking the obvious steps and leaving the rest to Divine Wisdom.

14

Visiting New York in the fall had become an annual event. I loved the city in early autumn. There seemed to be an air of freshness and new beginnings. Carol Ann and I arrived in mid-September. Polly and Annette planned to meet us. This year, I had scheduled two dinners in the Café as our group continued to grow. By now my interests had branched out beyond Christy to the fabulous history of the Hotel itself.

Carol Ann and I had a lunch date with John McDaniel, now Rosie O'Donnell's musical director. Carol Ann had met John some years earlier, and they had become good friends. They'd lost touch with each other, but when *The Rosie O'Donnell Show* appeared on TV, Carol Ann was thrilled to see his name in the credits.

The show was taped live at Rockefeller Center. John felt that we'd have more time together if we met him there. On the morning of our lunch, I woke up to find Carol Ann already in the sitting room. The TV was on.

"What's going on?" I felt a creeping anxiety.

"Believe it or not," she said, "Rockefeller Center is on fire."

I joined her on the sofa and saw the chaotic scene for myself. Fire trucks were stationed all around the Center. The streets were cordoned off from traffic, but bystanders milled about.

Only a month before we had watched a similar scene in Los Angeles when the Hollywood Studio Museum had also caught fire in the early hours of a Wednesday morning. The coincidence was eerie. Rockefeller Center sustained a great deal of smoke damage due to a mishap in the building's electrical system and would be closed for weeks of repair. The Today Show and Rosie O'Donnell would have to move to interim quarters.

"What now?" I asked.

"I guess I'll call John and leave a message. Maybe he'll call us soon."

Then there was nothing to do but watch the continuing news rundown and wait. An hour or more crept by, and at 9:30 the phone rang.

"I'm okay." John assured Carol Ann. "I've been busy returning calls to my family. I won't know for awhile whether we'll be working today or not, but I'll let you know when I get the word."

His second call came around eleven. "There's nothing we can do today," he said. "So lunch is on. I know a good restaurant only a block from your hotel. Let's meet there at noon. Actually, we'll have more time to be together than if all this hadn't happened."

Relieved and grateful, we walked the block to an Italian restaurant. Soon he walked in, smiling and handsome. We had a delightful two-hour lunch together, trading stories. Regis Philbin was seated several tables away. Fire or not, in New York, as in Hollywood, things had worked out with beautiful results.

Next we were off to meet Polly, Annette, and Carol—another Christy niece—at Ken Galenty's Silver Screen office. Ken owned a mass of artwork by American illustrators as well as photographs, letters, and historical data pertaining to them.

By Thursday evening we'd already had several sessions at the Hotel des Artistes. Artist Cecile Johnson had given us a tour of her home, presenting us with prints of her artwork. Her apartment boasted a massive stairway credited to Gutzon Borglum, the sculptor. She owned a Christy palette which she herself used.

We spent Thursday afternoon in the Hotel coffee shop, a small gem of a place, very European in feel and decor. Hiram Pagan and Dale Meyers Cooper joined us. Hiram had worked in the Café for decades and had received the "Best Waiter in New York" award. He'd been a close friend to both Nancy Christy and Fannie Hurst. Dale was a fine artist, as well as a beautiful and gracious lady. She had invited Carol Ann and me to visit her studio home in the Hotel the year before. Her apartment had once belonged to

Rudolph Valentino.

Earlier in the day I had placed several calls to David Halberstam. On the third try, I reached him. For years he'd lived just down the block from the Hotel des Artistes. Some time before he'd written an article for *Architectural Digest* titled "On the Street Where I Live." I knew he frequented the Café, and I hoped to get his feelings about the place.

On our last visit to New York in 1995, I had also called him. His secretary informed me that he'd left town just an hour earlier. At about midnight that night Carol Ann roused me from the sitting room. "Come in here quick!" David Halberstam was being interviewed on the Tom Snyder Late Night Show, an unexpected coincidence. I resolved to try again to reach the Pulitzer-Prize-winning author.

When I heard David's rich and resonant voice on the line, I plunged into an explanation of my call. His answers were articulate and informative. He loved visiting the coffee shop on the many afternoons when he walked his dog up and down West 67th St. "She's an item," he chuckled, "far better known in the neighborhood than I am."

He spoke of John Chancellor's death some months earlier. "When Jack died, a group of us decided to have a dinner in his honor at the Café, a wake, so to speak. We had my favorite table, the round one just inside the front door. It was a great evening. The Café has that wonderful ambiance, you know—warm and inviting and sophisticated at the same time. The murals are fabulous. So there we were, sharing stories and remembering our friend. There were farewell toasts and a lot of memories made that evening. I'll not forget it."

By 8:00 on Thursday evening, our group was in the Café at "the round table inside the front door." The three Christy nieces plus Walt and Mary Reed, Peter and Peggy Salwen, Carol Ann and I were given lavish attention by Hiram. It, too, was a night to remember.

Peter and Peggy had become dear friends. He was so supportive of my Christy dreams. Over and over he told me, "You can do it. I know you can."

Walt and Mary Reed

I called Walt early in the Christy Quest. I had discovered his excellent book, *Illustration in America,* and studied it diligently. Walt founded Illustration House in 1974, thus pioneering the market in illustration art. He was also an artist and knew many of the great illustrators.

It was with my usual sense of intimidation that I dialed his number at Illustration House. Surprisingly, he answered the phone. I told him how much I admired his book and asked if I might make an appointment to speak with him in person on my next trip to New York. "Of course," he said, "Come in anytime. I'll pull out the Christys we have." Walt was so affable and easy to talk to, my nervousness vanished with the conversation.

Since that first phone visit, I had gone to Illustration House during every New York trip, exploring the walls lined with well known works. Walt was a gentle man, as kind and considerate as he was knowledgeable. His wife, Mary, was often present and added her expertise as well. They were a delightful couple, and I treasured their friendship.

So another evening filled with friendship, laughter and stimulating conversation had come to a close. The Café dinners had become a cherished tradition.

The next morning Carol Ann and I met Polly, Annette and Carol at Marble Collegiate Church. By this time Dr. Peale had died and his portrait had been moved from the Peale Center to hang beside the one of his wife in the church parlor.

At 7:30 that evening, we gathered again in the Hotel des Artistes lobby. Olga breezed in, looking as lovely and young as ever. Joining us for the second time was Milton Justice. His father had been a dear friend and mentor to my mother and me since my father's death. Milton's career in the entertainment field had been forged at SMU. Bob Hope, who had generously endowed the University with a theater bearing his name, hired him as a member of his troupe when he graduated. A multi-talented writer and musician, Milton's expertise grew while living and working in California. He had been awarded both an Emmy and an Oscar in the same year, an unparalleled occurrence that spoke powerfully of his creative talent. Later, he moved to New York where he worked with Stella Adler and produced a Tennessee Williams' play on Broadway. He taught acting classes and loved instructing young theater students.

He filled us in on his latest venture: he was the producer of *Losing Chase*, a Showtime movie starring Helen Mirren, Beau Bridges, and Kyra Sedgwick. I sensed another Emmy in the wings.

After dinner as we toasted Annette's birthday, I thought again of Noel Coward's toast quoted in the Café cookbook, "A long life and happiness of us all."

It was near midnight when we rose from our table. The sense of Christy's presence was powerful. The artist's "playful hamadryads" as writer Brendan Behan termed them, frolicked across the Café wall just behind and above us. His Tarzan and Jane posed lifelike on the side mural. Christy's figures had reigned in the Café for over sixty years. It had now been a decade since I first fell under their spell.

"Come back soon," Hiram called out from a table across the room. "We'll be here, waiting for you."

After I returned to Dallas, Walt Reed called me one evening. "Helen, I have an interesting Christy painting here. I'm looking at it right now." I was intrigued. "Tell me about it."

"Well," he continued, "it happens to be a portrait of Christ." My heart skipped a beat. "I knew to call you," he was saying. "Do you know anything about it?"

"Walt, the portrait of Christ is what started me on the Christy Quest," I said. I told him about how the painting had surfaced ten years ago. "How in the world did it come to you?" I asked.

"It was sent to me for appraisal. It came from Tennessee, from Abingdon Press. I wanted some background information on it, so I called you," Walt answered.

"Maybe it's going back out on loan to another museum."

Walt affirmed the thought. "Probably so. The appraisal is likely for insurance purposes."

"I remain in awe about this whole process," I said. "I started out asking questions and now I'm answering them."

After I put down the telephone, I reflected again on the nature of the journey. There had been so many unexpected gifts along the way. I mentally added Walt's call to the growing store of what I felt were miracles.

The painting of Christ had reappeared. What would be its future?

On January 1, 1997, 1 wrote down my New Year's resolution, "Finish the book." I gave up trying to figure out where or how to end it and decided to let it happen spontaneously.

Carol Ann and I wanted to tour New England in the spring and planned a two-week trip for May. We'd fly to Boston, rent a car, and be on our way.

A month before our departure, I received a letter from Peter Harrington, Military Art Curator at Brown University in Providence, Rhode Island. He told me of the forthcoming Brown exhibit titled *"A Splendid Little War" The Spanish-American War, 1898, The Artists' Perspective.* Christy would be one of six American illustrators represented. Beginning in 1998, the exhibit would continue through the year. As a 100-year commemorative project, it would also tour the Eastern U.S. Walt Reed had referred Peter to me as a Christy researcher. Once again, graced by perfect timing, we set up an appointment for the day after our arrival in Boston.

We planned to visit Harvard University as well. There were

two Christy pastel portraits in the Harvard Theatre Collection: Ellen Terry as "Portia" and Ellen Drew as "Mrs. Malaprop" from *The Rivals*. The Christian Science Center owned two Christy portraits of Mary Baker Eddy. I wanted to drive to Medford and view "Olga's Angel." She had posed for the statue in the 1940s. Sculpted by an Italian artist, it was the powerful focal point in Oak Grove Cemetery.

Northampton was the site of the Forbes Library that housed Christy's portraits of President and Mrs. Coolidge. Deerfield Academy was close by and sported a drawing of Asa Bates by the artist.

Doris Styka and her daughter, Wanda, lived in the Stockbridge area. Wanda was an archivist for the Daniel Chester French Museum. Although Doris was tied up elsewhere, Wanda would be available to see us. The Styka connection had been one of the great miracles in the Christy Quest. I was most anxious to meet Jan Styka's granddaughter.

After leaving Stockbridge, we'd drive up to Pawlet, Vermont. Christy, Elise, and Holly had spent many summers at the Old Mill. Christy had refurbished the mill into a delightful vacation home and studio. We'd visit Nate Smith there. Nate and Holly had played together in their youth.

In March of 1997, 1 found myself gifted with a new secretary. I'd been lost without Melinda, who took a full-time job as a legal secretary in 1996. My files were a dismal mess, my correspondence was stacked up, and my inventory lay in uncoordinated piles. Rhonda suggested Judy Metzger, and she agreed to help me once a week. Judy was adept on the computer, creative, energetic and enthusiastic about the Christy Quest.

It quickly became apparent that Judy had a special knack. She was gifted in the art of dealing with people. Again and again, I heard: "What a delightful secretary you're blessed with!" "I hope to meet her in person," and "Your gracious secretary contacted me. . . . " I watched gratefully as she plowed through correspondence and brought inventory up to date. She was so much fun to be with, unfailingly upbeat and positive. I was convinced *The Christy Quest* could not be published without her. I loved her work, and more importantly, I loved her friendship and support.

Besides the Brown University exhibit, there were other enticing Christy projects underway. A Christy enthusiast named Sean West contacted me with plans to promote Christy's original oil painting later issued as a poster for railroad safety. A Washington, D.C. unveiling would commemorate the 125th anniversary of the artist's birth in January 1998. Sean, who lived in Virginia, was full of ideas. His eagerness was contagious and refreshing. He hoped to form a Christy network of all those interested in the artist. A Christy-gram would be printed and distributed in intervals during the year.

Another exciting development came from Washington in June. I received a call from Lincoln Oliphant who informed me that he was writing a book on Christy's great oil painting, *The Signing of the Constitution*. The curators at Annapolis had given him my name. I pledged to help and immediately delved into my files.

Urania wanted to explore the possibility of having a Christy stamp or stamp series approved by the U.S. Postal Department. Although she was inundated by requests for her artwork and held the presidency of the International Pastel Society, I knew how devoted she was to her dream. And I knew, too, that it would come about in its own ideal timing.

I wanted to continue to travel, research and catalogue the artist's work, and most of all, meet new Christy connections. At home, my walls bloomed with prints by American illustrators. Restoring and framing turn-of-the-century magazine covers, ads, posters and portraits had brought me so much pleasure. It was almost as though the faces, figures and events were alive again.

One day Judy called me with surprising news: "Helen, I just finished talking to Rosalyn Lewis with Abingdon Press about using the portrait of *The Christ* in your book. Guess who now owns the painting?"

I had heard nothing about the piece since Walt Reed called me for information about it.

"Ken Wapnick has it," Judy sang out. "It belongs to the Foundation for a Course in Miracles!"

My mind riveted on a single thought: *This is the closure for the Christy Quest.* The portrait had found its home. Destiny had delivered it to the place where the quest began.

I dialed Ken's office immediately. After I explained the reason for my call, his first words were, "Helen, I'm looking at *The Christ* as we speak. It is hanging opposite my desk." He told me that friends who attended his workshop had purchased it as a gift for him. During our conversation I realized again what an impact *The Course in Miracles* and the Christy Quest had made in my life. They had arrived together. It was impossible to separate them.

Ken invited me to visit the Miracles Foundation in Roscoe, New York. I knew I would do so when the time was right. I would stand once more before Christy's portrait of Christ.

I began to formulate the lessons I'd learned since I had begun the quest. I, who had experienced so much fear throughout most of my life, was learning the meaning of love and trust. The portrait of Christ had been the catalyst which prompted me to take risks into unknown territory. Ken told me there would be a third edition of his book, and this time the cover would be photographed from the original oil.

I felt a bit like a new edition myself. A guiding spirit had, in a sense, edited out the painful and non-working inner parts, replacing them with stretches of joy. The lessons were gentle. Each held an unexpected gift. The universe was benevolent; I had only to ask for help. As my mind opened, my heart followed suit. I began to trust in love rather than fear. No person, place or thing is unimportant in God's world. All events are interconnected, and the journey through life has no final result. The journey itself is the miracle. Though a circle may close, it is the joining of ends that empowers it to expand into infinity.

What had been the greatest gift of the quest? I had met people from all walks of life. Many from the world of art had become not only acquaintances, but also dear friends. Our New York Christy Circle had widened dramatically. I couldn't think of a city, place or area of the country where there was not a Christy connection. From coast to coast and in between, there had been support for *The Christy Quest.* With each new contact, a flood of information poured forth. I felt rich in experience and friendship.

It had now been over a dozen years since I first became intrigued with Howard Chandler Christy. Year by year and step by step, the Quest had unfolded. I had no reason to believe that it would not continue to express in the most remarkable ways. It was, after all, an adventure. . . .

ABOUT THE AUTHOR

Helen F. Copley, a graduate of Southern Methodist University, has lived in the Dallas area most of her life. She has three children—Julie, Ward, and Drew—and three grandchildren. She continues her research on Howard Chandler Christy, planning for a biography and a film documentary to appear in the near future.

It is the sunrise I love. I love the morning because it is new; it is the creation of life all over again. And I love to paint in the morning.

—Howard Chandler Christy

PICTURE CREDITS

Cover: *Howard Chandler Christy* by James Montgomery Flagg, 1919; Helen F. Copley, owner.

Back cover: Author photograph by Cheryl Masterson

Frontispiece: *Self Portrait* by Howard Chandler Christy, National Portrait Gallery, Smithsonian Institution, gift of Henry Ostrow, NPG.78.269

Page vi: Photo by David Pierce

Page 3: *The Christ* by Howard Chandler Christy, courtesy of Abingdon Press

Page 22: Photo by Andrew Alpern, courtesy of Dover Publications

Page 33: *My Sidekick* by Howard Chandler Christy, courtesy of the Ohio Historical Society

Page 56: Photo courtesy of Holly Longuski

Page 57: *Holly* by Howard Chandler Christy; photo courtesy of the Archives of the American Illustrators Gallery, New York City, © 1999, by AsaP of Holderness, N H 03245 USA

Page 81: *The Dance* © 1903, Chas. Scribner's Sons, New York

Page 86: Photo by the author

Page 112: Navy Girl by Howard Chandler Christy, 1917

Page 115: *For Thine Is The Kingdom* by Howard Chandler Christy; photo courtesy of the Archives of the American Illustrators Gallery, New York City © 1999, by AsaP of Holderness, NH 03245 USA

Page 122: Portrait of Miss Ethelyn Sarratt Talbott, 1938 by Howard Chandler Christy, Georgia Museum of Art, University of Georgia; gift of Maj. Gen. A. W. Kissner, Springfield, VA, GMOA 72.2779

Page 127: Photo by Carol Ann Kendrick

Page 139: Photo by Hiram Pagan

Page 148: *Teasing* © 1905, Moffat, Yard & Co., New York. Photo courtesy of Darlene McNaughton.

Page 149: Portrait of Dorothy Thomas by Howard Chandler Christy, courtesy of Zanesville Art Center

Page 154: Photo by Carol Ann Kendrick

Page 164: Photo by Carol Ann Kendrick

Page 173: Photo by Carol Ann Kendrick

Page 180: Photo by Carol Ann Kendrick

With sincere thanks to my editor, Dr. Betty Burnett, for her guidance, patience, and support. She skillfully wove the details of the Quest into a delightful whole, making my dream a reality.